Praise for

OUTSMARTING EGOMANIACS

"What do I have to say about Carla's amazing new book? Wow! Well done! *Outsmarting Egomaniacs* is well written, well organized, interesting, informative, novel, *AND* entertaining!"

—Iona Monk, MA, creator of the podcast *Relationship Dish*

"Within the pages of this book lies a treasure trove of knowledge, presented in a structure so seamless, accessible, concise, and impeccably organized that it makes managing narcissistic personalities feel like second nature. Its user-friendly layout renders it a breeze to navigate, whether you're a seasoned psychologist or a curious layperson. But what truly sets this book apart is its practicality. Each chapter is a roadmap, guiding you through the complexities of psychology with clarity and precision. Whether you're seeking insights into human behavior or practical tips for everyday life, you'll find exactly what you need.

I was captivated by its irreverent and conversational tone, which infuses every page with a refreshing charm. Carla is direct and unfiltered. This is not just a book—it's a companion, guiding you through the labyrinth of the mind with wit and wisdom. You are less alone with this portable therapist in the palm of your hand.

Having had the privilege of training with Carla, I can attest firsthand to her brilliance as a therapist. Her insights, wisdom, and unwavering dedication to her craft are nothing short of remarkable. In these pages, you'll encounter Carla's expertise distilled into its purest form—a testament to her passion for helping others comprehend the complexities of the human experience and respond in a manner that betters their lives."

—Michele Goldberg, LMFT, founder of
Find Your Center Therapy

Outsmarting
Egomaniacs

CARLA LITTO, LMFT

Outsmarting Egomaniacs

HOW TO RESPOND TO NARCISSISTS AND MASTER MANIPULATORS

WONDERWELL

Published by Wonderwell Press
Austin, Texas
www.gbgpress.com

Distributed by Greenleaf Book Group

For ordering information or special discounts for bulk purchases, please contact Greenleaf Book Group at PO Box 91869, Austin, TX 78709, 512.891.6100.

Design and composition by Greenleaf Book Group and Brian Phillips
Cover design by Greenleaf Book Group and Brian Phillips
Cover images: © rangizzz and AOME1812. Used under license from Shutterstock.com

Publisher's Cataloging-in-Publication data is available.

Print ISBN: 978-1-963827-00-2

eBook ISBN: 978-1-963827-01-9

To offset the number of trees consumed in the printing of our books, Greenleaf donates a portion of the proceeds from each printing to the Arbor Day Foundation. Greenleaf Book Group has replaced over 50,000 trees since 2007.

Printed in the United States of America on acid-free paper

24 25 26 27 28 29 30 31   10 9 8 7 6 5 4 3 2 1

First Edition

This book is dedicated to those who inspired it
and probably will not read it.

CONTENTS

DISCLAIMER

The names of clients and other individuals in this book, along with their identifying details, have been changed to protect their privacy.

While the book's subject, the Egomaniac, can be male or female, I have chosen to use the pronouns he/him in general cases where there is no specific subject for simplicity.

The information in this book is not a substitute for individual therapy and is not intended to be used to develop formal diagnoses. If you feel the information in this book is relevant to you or someone in your life, I urge you to seek out a licensed mental health professional.

If you are in a domestic violence situation or your partner is physically abusive and you fear that you are in imminent danger, consult with a counselor or therapist or contact a domestic violence hotline to ensure your safety.

WHO ARE EGOMANIACS, NARCISSISTS, AND MASTER MANIPULATORS?

What Is an Egomaniac?

An egomaniac is a self-absorbed, egocentric individual who invariably pisses off almost everyone around him because of his intolerable obsession with himself, which precludes his ability to see things from the perspective of others.

What Is a Narcissist?

Many egomaniacs are raging narcissists. All narcissists are egomaniacs, but not all egomaniacs are necessarily full-blown narcissists. The two terms can be used interchangeably, but narcissists have more advanced exploitation skills and completely lack empathy.

Let's talk about narcissists for a minute, since narcissism is such a hot button lately. People are obsessed with this word because they are finally, for maybe the first time in their lives, discovering that there is an actual label to describe the "crazy" person in their lives. On the one hand, this is great. Learning about this disorder can be eye-opening and help you process things like the fact that you can't fix or change your disturbed loved one. On the other hand, some people are using this word to describe anyone who hurts them, and in some cases as a way to free themselves of any accountability in the relationship and play the victim. Projection maybe? We'll discuss manipulation tactics later in the book. For now, suffice to say, narcissism is real. It's slippery. And tricky. It's something you want to have in your life about as much as you want to roll around in a bed full of broken glass. So, what is narcissism, exactly?

Narcissists are self-absorbed, pride-protecting, empathy-lacking, greed-driven individuals who hurt other people to protect their fragile egos and maintain their status as superior, special, or perfect. They are more dangerous than ordinary egomaniacs and random assholes because they tend to be skilled master manipulators.

What Is a Master Manipulator?

Some manipulative people earn the title of master manipulator because they are so skilled at manipulation that they catch you unaware. Their manipulation is slow and insidious. You might not realize what is happening until you find yourself deep in the trenches of their insanity. You might feel helpless, hopeless, and stuck. By the time you realize you are stuck in their grip, you might feel like there is no right answer and nowhere to turn. You might be madly in love with this person who is enslaving you to their one-sided, distorted reality, or you might be plotting to run for the hills while shaking in fear about how this person will turn your life upside down once you escape. Either way, they've got you by the tail.

Why Does It Matter?

When you get too close to a toxic person, it wears you down, beats you into submission, and sends you spiraling into self-doubt. You find yourself second-guessing your every move, everything from *should I ditch this guy?* to *what kind of protein should I be putting on my salad?* Unrelenting self-doubt leads to depression and anxiety.

As Lori Gottlieb, author of *Maybe You Should Talk to Someone*, quotes on social media from her book, "Before diagnosing someone with depression, make sure they aren't surrounded by assholes." And yet the world is full of assholes. A remarkable variety of assholes roam freely on this earth, so chances are you've encountered more than one. This book delineates all the different types of difficult, toxic, and manipulative people who destroy relationships, and they all have at least one thing in common: their toxic behavior is governed by an ego that is massive and fragile and simultaneously overpowering and insurmountable.

Maybe you've been on a date with an arrogant egomaniac, worked long hours for an ungrateful control freak, or gotten scammed by a con artist. Chances are, if you are reading this book, you currently feel stuck in a toxic relationship with someone who is hurting you, manipulating you, controlling you, lying to you, or behaving in ways that make no sense. Trying to understand this person is like trying to solve the most annoying puzzle ever. Worst of all, you feel powerless under their reign.

Why I Wrote This Book

I have been a marriage and family therapist in Los Angeles for more than a decade, although I have always considered myself to be some kind of therapist in training from an early age. As both a therapist and a human being, I have been there, and I have seen it all. I have seen people get catfished and conned. I have seen family members steal written wills, inheritances, and family trusts from their own siblings, parents, and children. I have seen romantic partners lead double lives, pretend to be someone else for long periods of time, or fake terminal cancer. I have seen planned "oopsie" pregnancies entrap scared men and suicide threats keep miserable spouses from leaving. This list is endless.

To varying degrees and at different times in our lives, we have all been, or will be, exposed to toxic behavior, whether it matches the magnitude of the previous descriptions or not. I was raised in a highly dysfunctional family, and my childhood and early adult experiences have kept me infinitely curious about human behavior and have, in many ways, shaped who I am today. Events I witnessed in my life definitely influenced my life purpose. My own personal experiences with narcissistic individuals, combined with my education and extensive training as a therapist, led me to specialize in narcissistic abuse recovery, co-dependency, and high-conflict relationship issues. I have spent well over a decade helping people manage or break free from these unfortunate relationships.

My ability to intuitively assess people and instantly identify manipulation tactics brings swift clarity to my clients in therapy sessions. When I am conducting a therapy session with my clients who are struggling to stand up for themselves, they frequently stop me and begin writing my words down as I am giving them the tools and, especially, the words they can use to help themselves. Some of my clients have said to me, "I wish I could plant a device with you in my ear when I am arguing with this person." I created this book so that you, and every person sharing this struggle, will always have a guide and be able to keep me in your ear.

If you are in a domestic violence situation or your partner is physically abusive and you fear that you are in imminent danger, consult with a therapist or counselor to create a safety plan, or contact a domestic violence hotline to ensure your safety.

What's In This Book?

This book is designed to help you make sense of what is occurring by deconstructing your egomaniac's psychology in plain language so you can identify their egocentric toxic behavior and manipulation tactics. You will find descriptions of the different types of manipulators and the manipulation tactics each type tends to use, as well as tips and tools to protect yourself. As you read each description, I hope you will recognize your own special egomaniac and understand their psychology with more clarity than ever.

The first part of this book explains the spectrum of narcissism and covers the variety of manipulation tactics that anyone might use on you. Many people today are familiar with terms like *gaslighting*, which is just one of the many manipulation tactics out there. All the different forms of manipulation are covered in this book to help you easily recognize which ones apply to you.

Part 2 takes you on a tour of the many different types of egomaniacs you might encounter. This book creates categories—but not to put people in boxes, because individuals almost never fit into neat categories. Instead, these categories are designed to connect you to your personal experience and make it easier for you to identify your toxic person or manipulator. You are not alone in what you see, feel, and experience. When you read each chapter on the different types of egomaniacs, you might find that yours is a combination of two or three of them. Some very special egomaniacs might fall into every single category, and that means you are dealing with someone remarkably disturbed, so keep reading. Yes, this book can help you with even the most disturbed, dysfunctional, and toxic people.

Most importantly, this book will teach you how to outsmart every different kind of egomaniac you might find yourself involved with, even the most masterfully manipulative. How do you outsmart the cunning fox? Well, it's not by acting like the fox. First, you need to understand the fox. But you also need to understand yourself so you comprehend why the fox has chosen you and how you are serving that fox.

In combat, for example, often the biggest or physically strongest person is not necessarily the one who wins. The person with more skills will usually beat their tougher opponents. In my spare time, I practice Brazilian jiu-jitsu. I recommend martial arts training to all my clients who are working on growing their confidence and most especially to those who are suffering from complex PTSD after enduring an abusive relationship.

Brazilian jiu-jitsu, a martial art growing in popularity, is about using technique, not strength, to defeat your opponent. This art teaches techniques that result in the ability to exert control over your opponent regardless of their size or strength. If you find this hard to believe, simply scroll on your social media and you will find videos like the Brazilian jiu-jitsu–trained woman who choked out four men in a row at a boxing gym. All of them had been convinced that a woman could never choke them out. Until all four of them tapped, within seconds. That is a perfect example of technique and skill over size and strength. The point here is this: The loudest voice does not always win, the biggest ego does not always shine, and the biggest asshole is not necessarily the one taking home the prize. Not when you can outsmart them.

Outsmarting your manipulator is only part of what we are learning to do in this book. You will also learn what you have control over when you are feeling defeated and hopeless, which battles to fight, and which ones aren't worth fighting. After developing insights about both yourself and your manipulator in part 2, part 3 arms you with a sturdy voice, sharp comebacks, and firm boundary-setting techniques. This section provides thought-provoking reflections for you to use to evaluate your relationship in the same way you might be guided to do in a therapy session.

The final section of this book, part 4, is about building your new life with confidence and surrounding yourself with healthy, balanced relationships. The purpose of this book is to help you cultivate fulfilling relationships and reduce your exposure to egomaniacs so you can enjoy your life. Egomaniacs will always exist, of course, but you can learn how to stay one step ahead of them, skillfully manage them, or distance yourself from them so you can live a happy life with peace and serenity instead of drama and bullshit.

PART ONE

Egomaniacs Come with a Bag of Tricks

Chapter 1

EGOMANIA: ON THE SPECTRUM OF NARCISSISM

THE MAJORITY OF MY CLIENTS WHO MEET with me to sort out their tumultuous love lives start out wanting to know whether their partner is a narcissist. Most of my clients are women who want to know whether the guy in their lives who is acting like an asshole meets the criteria to be diagnosed with the disorder. I ask them, what would his diagnosis do for you? What does it mean to you that he's a narcissist? Without hesitation, they say because then I'll know for sure that I should definitely leave him! My response is, okay, but does he have to be a full-blown narcissist in order for you to leave him? Isn't being an asshole enough?! They invariably come back with, well, you're the one who said that narcissists are incapable of change. That is true. And yet, the crux of the matter boils down to this: My clients repeatedly express the same strong sense of hope—that their partner will change. He may or may not be a full-blown narcissist (I can't technically diagnose someone who is not present), although the descriptions given by my clients often include many narcissistic traits and behaviors. But more importantly, the actual diagnosis of the partner is of little concern. A diagnosis is not all that tells us someone's capacity for change. The actions and words of my clients' partners speak volumes about whether they are willing to change. There is no need to determine whether a partner is a certifiable narcissist or just a plain asshole who's not willing to change, or even in some cases, just a regular dude who isn't meeting his partner's needs and is never going to. Instead, I focus on my clients and what *they* can change. In this book, we'll focus on what is happening to you, and what you can do about it.

The first step toward any kind of change is identifying the problem. If a person is ever going to change at all, they have to be able to first recognize their own bullshit. At the very least, they must be able to see how their own behavior, issues, or emotional baggage is getting in the way of their happiness or your happiness together. They have to be able to acknowledge how they are part of the problem. Next, they need to be willing to do something about it. If you are dealing with someone who can't even arrive at that initial stage of problem-solving, then hanging on and hoping the person will change is like wishing in one hand and taking a giant crap in the other hand and seeing which one fills up first.

I will give you this much—if your partner cannot tolerate hearing your experience when it involves recognizing his behavior, he most likely does sit somewhere on the spectrum of narcissism. If apologies are nonexistent or sound like lame-ass excuses for an apology because they are embedded in defensive language, and somehow the blame is pointed back at you, then yeah, he doesn't sound like a guy who's about to change and get right to work on fixing your relationship. In the end, if he's not willing to do some self-reflection and hold himself accountable for his behavior, then ultimately, we need to talk about you, not him. What do you want, what do you need, and what are you prepared to do? For yourself, not him.

One of the principles in Brazilian jiu-jitsu is that when you can't move your bigger, heavier opponent, you move yourself around him instead. This is a great analogy for a life concept that we will be exploring more in this book: The only realistic form of control is self-control. That is why this book will also help you increase your self-awareness, which will help you do a better job of being strategic about your own moves. We will get there in part 3. But for now, let's get familiar with the spectrum.

The Spectrum of Narcissism

How do you know whether someone has Narcissistic Personality Disorder (NPD)?

> Narcissistic Personality Disorder: (n) one of the few conditions in which the patient is left alone and everyone else is treated

Ha! This little joke has more than a nugget of truth, but here's a more serious, accurate, clinical, and thorough definition: NPD is a serious mental illness that disrupts the person's mood, self-identity, behavior, relationships, and personal growth. Narcissism is characterized by self-absorbed and empathy-deficient traits, like the ones briefly described in the following.

Grandiosity, which is all about their need for you to notice how important they are. Maybe they brag a lot, but also maybe they just make shit up. I have a narcissistic relative who announces at every holiday gathering that ten million dollars is arriving any day now from the special business deal he made. He's been saying that for the last four years—"any day now!" When the narcissist believes their own bullshit, it's called *magical thinking*. Narcissists live in a fantasy world. Everything they say and do is designed to support this fantasy. Their appetite for admiration is endless. Their inevitable envy of others can be dark and dangerous.

They are *arrogant, self-entitled, and prone to rage*, particularly when things aren't going their way. Just imagine a rotten, bratty toddler in an adult's body, and now you have the picture. Convinced they are special or superior to others, they demand special treatment. They *exploit and manipulate* others, doing whatever it takes to meet their end goals, and they do it *without a shred of empathy*. If it feels like it's always about them, that's because it is.

Narcissism is an affliction shared by the narcissistic individual as well as the people who love, live with, work with, care about, and are dependent on the narcissist. Unfortunately, there is no cure, no remedy, no pill to reverse the direction this condition takes, which tends to worsen with age. NPD is only marginally treatable at best, if at all, due to the narcissist's limited capacity for self-reflection. Their inability to change is why learning how to protect yourself is so important.

Narcissism exists on a spectrum. At one end of the spectrum is healthy narcissism, where you find confident, outgoing people who know how to take care of themselves while still showing compassion for others. I use the word healthy because this is where we should all strive to be, in an ideal balance of caring about ourselves as well as others. Narcissism in this context is not the toxic kind we are usually talking about.

Further along the spectrum is where you might find egomaniacs —your average garden-variety assholes and energy suckers who exhibit some narcissistic traits, rendering them annoying and maybe even intolerable in high doses. At the far end of the spectrum are full-blown narcissists who exhibit enough narcissistic traits to meet the criteria for NPD. These people are disturbed individuals who thrive on their ability to control, manipulate, and exploit other human beings. Additionally, I believe Antisocial Personality Disorder, the disorder that accounts for sociopaths (the people capable of the most inhumane crimes), is an extension of the narcissism spectrum at the most disturbed end; it surpasses NPD. Sometimes it is hard to know where to draw the line across the spectrum.

Healthy levels of narcissism (ideal confidence)	• Confident yet humble, willing to admit mistakes or flaws • Strives for self-improvement and values constructive criticism • Engages in self-care while also caring about others' needs • Prioritizes self but also knows when to value the "good of the whole" and takes into consideration others' feelings • Does not compare self to others
Your average narcissistic individual (Egomaniac)	• Appears overly confident, often brags, likes to be "right" • Has a hard time taking in criticism of any kind • Might at times be bossy, controlling, selfish, etc. yet is sometimes capable of recognizing this and even apologizing • Can be manipulative to get their way • Often jealous of others
Full-blown Narcissistic Personality Disorder (danger zone)	• Arrogant rather than confident, always "right" • Bragging is blown out of proportion, even potentially delusional • Compares self to others, belittles others, spreads false rumors • Defends against criticism, no capacity for self-reflection • Self-absorbed, dominant, and controlling behavior is consistent and severe (to the point of many severed ties or cut-offs) • Relies callously on manipulation and exploitation to get their way • Bitter jealousy and dark envy consume them • Preoccupied with seeking revenge on others

The purpose of this spectrum is to present the full range of possibilities, including those unclear, gray areas of where to draw the line between redeemable and narcissist. The line doesn't have to be clear, but being able to conceptualize a range of behaviors is helpful. It helps to know, as you read this book and understand who you are dealing with, approximately how far down the spectrum your person deviates from the healthy range. The closer your person gets to the full-blown NPD category, the more likely you should run for the hills.

The healthy range at the top is where you want to be, and where you can only hope all your friends and family will land. We all want to be and to surround ourselves with kind, caring people. We are also attracted to confidence, and naturally, we want to be confident ourselves. Confidence, or self-worth, is not narcissism in the way we generally talk about narcissism as toxic. People frequently confuse confidence and self-worth with narcissism and its traits of arrogance, self-aggrandizement, and self-entitlement. This spectrum of narcissism marks a distinction between confidence and arrogance.

Truly confident people are able to accept their flaws instead of presenting a façade of superiority and perfection to the outside world. Confident people welcome constructive criticism, and narcissists perpetually defend against it. Confident people don't compare themselves to others and don't feel the need to belittle anyone. Confident people don't get overly defensive at the slightest perception of criticism because confident people know who they are, which means nobody can come along and shake their self-image. They are humble, not insecure. Their strong sense of self minimizes their risk of being targets of manipulation. Read that last sentence again. This is why your confidence is paramount to defending against and shielding yourself from manipulation, which we will cover in more depth in later chapters.

Narcissists, by contrast, are emotionally stunted adults with the moral development of toddlers. They are continually testing boundaries, grasping for praise, and becoming unglued when they don't get their way. The average unhealthy narcissist, the one most people are likely to encounter, usually appears harmless at first glance. You might, at least initially, mistake the egomaniac's bravado for confidence. Over time, as you get closer, you begin to see their narcissistic tendencies seeping out. They might not swindle a pile of cash from you or send a hitman to your front porch, but their self-centered, manipulative behavior will still hurt. Narcissistic abuse is the kind of insidious emotional damage that is barely detectable yet gradually chips away at the self-esteem of its victims.

A full-blown personality disorder usually indicates that a person has many of the traits associated with the disorder and that the traits exist at a level severe enough to cause impairment in their life. Ten personality disorders are listed in the *Diagnostic and Statistical Manual of Mental Health Disorders* (DSM). Clinically speaking, to meet the criteria for NPD, which accounts for a small percentage of the general population, the individual would need to meet at least five of the nine criteria listed in the DSM that cause life-functioning impairment. What do I mean by impairment?

Impairment can look like, for example, not being able to keep a job. People with NPD often quit their jobs, or they keep getting fired for insubordination or not getting along with their coworkers. On the flip side, they might fire others frequently if they have the power to do so. They are not able to sustain close, personal relationships, and they tend to experience family conflict severe enough to result in cut ties. They go through friendships like toilet paper. Eventually, they burn bridges and make enemies everywhere they go. Here is the nutshell version of this: When a person can't get along at home, at work, or with anyone else who gets close enough to their bullshit, narcissism is probably driving their dysfunctional behavior. This person is most likely the common denominator to all their "problems" without ever knowing it.

Again, though, who cares whether narcissism is diagnosable or not. What we care about in this book is identifying the narcissistic behavior and manipulation tactics that egomaniacs and narcissists might be using on you, so you can protect yourself with the right skills and tools. The best way to shield yourself from toxic people is to spot them coming from miles away so you don't get sucked in. If you've already gotten sucked in, this book will help you examine who you are dealing with and help you decide what to do about it. The first thing we are going to do in this book is fine-tune your asshole antennae and supercharge your bullshit detector. On that note, let's deepen (no pun intended) our knowledge of assholes, or more specifically, egomaniacs and narcissists.

How Are Egomaniacs Created? The Narcissistic Wound

The first thing people seem to want to know is whether narcissists are born this way or become this way. Both. First of all, NPD is a personality disorder, which means the budding baby narcissist was born with a certain amount of genetic material that was conducive to forming a narcissistic personality; however, the environment plays an equally significant role in shaping that child. Almost anytime you find yourself in the nature-versus-nurture debate, the result is going to be a combination of both, in my opinion. The personality a child is gifted with in combination with a certain type of environment is what shapes that child's development. In sum, inherent narcissistic traits that are positively reinforced by the baby narcissist's caretakers will have the most pronounced effect.

By now, you are probably wondering, yikes, what do parents do to reinforce narcissistic behavior? If parents play a role in the development of a narcissist, what does that look like? It could go a few different ways. But first, let's learn the term *narcissistic wound*.

Although the grown-up narcissist presents a stellar façade to the outside world, deep down inside lives a fragile, attention-seeking, wounded child. This narcissistic wound, also referred to as the narcissistic injury, refers to the seemingly irrational reaction presented when a narcissist feels criticized or attacked. Where does this wound come from? The child's family history can create this wound in many ways, and there are many explanations for the development of such a raw, fragile ego.

Attachment Theory

Studies in attachment theory have shown that children with parents and caregivers who are attentive and consistent are more likely to develop a secure attachment style. Alternatively, children with inattentive, neglectful, and inconsistent caregivers are more likely to develop insecure attachment styles that reflect anxiety, avoidance, or a combination of both. People who grew up with insecure attachment styles cope with their feelings of insecurity and inadequacy by seeking validation and praise from the external environment and have an overdeveloped sense of self-importance. This external source is commonly referred to as narcissistic supply, which is essentially the attention and energy self-absorbed people suck out of others.

In simpler terms, when at least one parent or caregiver is unempathetic, emotionally unavailable, or neglectful, the child is left emotionally starved, which causes the child to develop a reliance on their external world (validation from others) instead of their internal world (their sense of self). Without a developing sense of self, they rely on others to validate their self-worth. This means they might, as a consequence, become insular and self-absorbed, seeking admiration from others to fill their supply. Children who do not learn how to develop their internal world and process their feelings of shame risk developing narcissistic traits as a coping mechanism.

I want to emphasize that although narcissists lack a secure attachment style, not all insecure attachment styles are indicative of narcissism. Insecure attachment styles, a result of inconsistent, neglectful, or abusive caregivers, indicate a maladaptive style of coping, whether or not the individual exhibits narcissistic traits. Narcissism is the result of the genetic predisposition of a narcissistic personality in combination with an insecure attachment style.

Settings That Breed Burgeoning Baby Narcissists

A narcissistic wound can develop within a narcissistically prone child in at least a couple of different ways. The following are two contrasting settings that could produce the same result.

The narcissistic individual's intense reactivity to feeling attacked or criticized can sometimes be traced back to a time in the young child's life when he felt unbearable shame or humiliation that he never fully recovered from. This child might have endured enormous pressure from highly critical, perhaps even abusive, parents who pushed him to excel without tolerance for any mistakes or missteps. This child develops a crucial need to perform without failure to avoid a beating. The parents might say the following statements: What do you mean you got an A- in trigonometry? Why didn't you score that goal? What is wrong with you? Don't be a loser. Why aren't you perfect? Ahhhh! That kind of parent. Remember Jamie Tartt in season one of the television series *Ted Lasso*, when his loudmouthed, drunk, dickhead dad comes to visit him after a game? That was the moment when we learn how Jamie's massive ego was grown, and we develop more compassion for the character who is able to evolve in later seasons.

In contrast to this upbringing, and the more common situation, is a spoiled child who was allowed to live in his star-like bubble at all times. This, of course, fails to present a realistic view of the world and fosters a deep sense of entitlement in the child. These parents cushioned their precious child from any discomfort the real world has to offer. These are the enabling parents who don't discipline their perfect, amazing child. Instead, they make excuses for him and shield him from the consequences of his own actions. How many times have we seen the mother in a documentary or true crime drama talk about her serial killer son as a "good boy" to the police? That kind of parent.

In either situation, toddler-aged children navigate the world during an egocentric phase of life, which is a normal, necessary, and transitional phase requiring the guidance of attuned caregivers. During this crucial phase, a child learns how to tolerate disappointment and self-soothe with the help of attuned parents and appropriate role models, and the child can develop a more balanced view of himself with regard to others. In contrast, if the child is flooded with incomprehensible shame or unrealistically protected from it, an ego-driven, shame-deflecting self-entitled monster is grown.

The narcissist, deep down, is essentially a wounded child reaching for admiration, the spotlight, and praise from everyone around him to restore his flawless self-image, which he counts on for survival. Like a bottomless well, a single person is not capable of filling the wounded person's supply at all times. To the narcissist, this endless validation is his lifeline. Other people are the means to fill his supply, and when they fail to perform, the narcissist reverts to that helpless childlike state and spirals into an emotional tantrum. The narcissistic wound is considered the root cause of the narcissist's infantile rage state, distorted self-image, and stunted capacity for empathy. The narcissist is always looking to fill his supply by gathering praise because the absence of it might force him to realize his deficiencies or shameful truths about himself, which is an experience he cannot bear.

But What If I'm the Crazy One?

People often find themselves in therapy to deal with and heal from the people in their lives who either won't go to therapy or whom therapy can't help.

"I need to meet with a narcissist specialist," Kaylee blurted out the moment I returned her call. When I get inquiries from people seeking a specialist in NPD, it is usually because they are married to one, divorcing one, breaking up with one, were raised by one, or can't get away from one. They rarely report that they think they might be one themselves. On the rare occasion that this happens, my curiosity is piqued. True narcissists typically do not seek therapy as self-declared narcissists who want to change. They don't consider themselves to be part of the problem, and they don't admit to needing help or needing to change a single thing about themselves. If they do seek therapy, often it's a way to merely complain about someone else and blame the world at large for their shitty existence without recognizing themselves as the common denominator in all their messes. For this reason, I almost always suspect the opposite is true—that these people calling me to find out whether they are, in fact, a narcissist, are the victims. They are being manipulated by a narcissist who is convincing them that they are the sole problem in their toxic relationship.

Despite my strong hunch that I might already know the answer, I asked Kaylee this question anyway: What makes you think you might be a narcissist? I waited for her to tell me that her boyfriend had accused her of being a narcissist and that she would like to find out whether it was true. After several sessions together, I began to learn about the relational dynamic between Kaylee and her boyfriend. While they both seemed to have their own interpersonal issues that were affecting their relationship, Kaylee's willingness in our sessions to self-reflect, learn how to listen better, and improve her communication style convinced me that I was not talking to a narcissist. She reported to me that even after she owned her part, apologized when it was appropriate, listened without getting defensive, and did everything on her end to repair their rapport, she felt like she was hitting a wall and nothing changed. Her boyfriend continued to play the victim and often resorted to social media to publicly lodge his complaints about her (a typical narcissist behavior). It became increasingly clear to me that she was dealing with a manipulator who was not capable of or willing to see his role in any of their problems. Casting her as the crazy one allowed him to escape accountability. This is a classic manipulation tactic. People in toxic relationships with toxic people often ask themselves this question at some point: Wait, what if I'm the crazy one?

If your relationship feels remarkably different from other relationships you've experienced, and if it feels like you are being driven crazy, that is because you most likely are actually being driven crazy. It's like you are letting a madman drive the bus and you're a passenger waiting to pass though Crazyville unscathed. You have not been driven crazy because you are a crazy person; you feel crazy because you are immersed in the world of a crazy person who is forcing their distorted reality on you.

Of course, I can't say for sure that whoever is holding this book is not an egomaniac or a narcissist or a manipulator or some form of crazy. Chances are, if you are searching for clues on how to deal with the difficult people in your life who are driving you crazy and harming you without reprieve, then I can say with a good amount of conviction that the information in this book will help you, especially if you are willing to do your own self-reflecting. Also, keep in mind, narcissists manipulate all different kinds of people—and that doesn't exclude other narcissistic people or people with some narcissistic traits as well. Just like when con artists themselves get conned, it's because they got conned by a better con artist.

The Egomaniac and Narcissist Behavior Catalog

The Narcissist's Club rules: That didn't happen. And if it did, it wasn't that bad. And if it was, it's not a big a deal. And if it is, it's not my fault. And if it was, I didn't mean it. And if I did, you deserved it. Thanks for playing!

Here is a checklist to help you determine whether you are dealing with an egomaniac or a narcissist. If you answer yes to a good number of these questions, it's time to reevaluate the relationship, and you should definitely keep reading this book.

They dominate conversations and situations.

- Do they talk almost exclusively about themselves?
- When you finally do talk about yourself, do they frequently top your story with a better one or immediately bring the conversation back to themselves?
- Do they become uncomfortable when they are not the center of attention?
- Do they frequently butt into plans, change plans they were invited to, or insist the plans go their way?
- Do they become strangely upset or enraged when things don't go their way?
- Do they expect you to constantly prioritize them over everyone else?
- Do they control who you talk to and see? Or what you're allowed to read and watch on TV? (That might sound crazy, but my client's girlfriend did exactly that.)
- Do they become irrationally jealous of other close relationships and try to restrict your access to them? Or guilt you for spending time with these people?

- Has their possessive nature led to isolation from the people you used to see more often?

They require excessive admiration.

- Do they boast and brag relentlessly?
- Do they exaggerate their talents and skills? Maybe even just make shit up?
- Are they an amazing storyteller, but you wonder what's real and what's fiction?
- Do they talk excessively about themselves as the star, the hero, or the martyr in almost every story?
- Does every story and situation cast them as special, unique, or favorable in some way?
- Are they preoccupied with looking better than everyone else?
- Are they obsessed with labels, such as work titles, and name-dropping?
- Do you find yourself cringing at the flashy nature of their social media pages?
- Do they frequently put others down or spread mean gossip?
- Do you worry they might make a scene or embarrass you in some way?
- Does this person behave like a world-class drama queen?

They are self-entitled and must get their way.

- Do they expect to receive special treatment?

- Do they play the victim in order to get special treatment or attention?

- Do they react defensively to fair criticism?

- Do they take advantage of others?

- Do they steal?

- Do they steal and then justify their stealing with a narrative about what they deserve?

- Do they lack empathy?

- Are they a shitty listener?

- Does it seem as though they don't care about your feelings?

- Do you feel ignored, neglected, or invisible around them?

- Are they unwilling to see things from your perspective?

- Is it difficult to get them to listen to you even when you tell them it's important?

- Do they belittle you?

- Do they use demeaning sarcasm to put you in your place?

- Do they laugh or brush you off when you tell them they hurt your feelings? Or label you too sensitive after they've been cruel?

- Does it seem impossible to get your needs met in this relationship?

- Do they manipulate you?

- Do you feel pressured or forced to do things you don't wish to do?

- Do you worry that you will be punished for saying no or disagreeing with them?

- Does it often feel like just agreeing to their demands is easier than starting a battle you can't win?

- Do you often suspect that you are being lied to?

- Do you intuitively feel like you're being manipulated?

- Do you worry what might happen if you don't give them what they want?

- Do you worry about what they might say about you to mutual friends, family, and others?

- Have you ever been told that what you know you saw or heard didn't actually happen?

If this list sounded all too familiar to you, then you might be asking yourself this question: I know this isn't normal, so why have I been putting up with this? There is more than one explanation.

When you have had positive experiences with this person in the past, those experiences seem to contradict everything you are experiencing now. You have grown attached to this person, or you felt in the past that you could trust this person, so when the manipulation starts, not only is it hard to believe, but it is also hard to accept. Social psychologists call this cognitive dissonance, which means that what you are experiencing contradicts what you know to be true. It's like smoking cigarettes even though you learned it causes cancer. Cognitive dissonance explains why you can't stop eating donuts even though you would like to be able to see your toes or zip your pants. It's way too uncomfortable for the brain to reconcile those two things, so you ignore or mentally fight against the contradictory information in front of you. Maybe you have somehow convinced yourself that this behavior is normal.

Another explanation is trauma bonding, which develops from

cycles of abuse followed by positive reinforcement; these cycles condition you to stay for the good times, which come and go. Cycles of abuse continue to fuel your need for validation and affection from your abuser in order to restore those positive feelings. Receiving their love again feels like a shot of heroin. You have become programmed to walk on eggshells around your abuser and prioritize pleasing them as you begin to place more value on the relationship than on caring for yourself. More on this in part 3 when we delve into self-awareness.

But perhaps even more important than uncovering your reasons for putting up with this treatment is asking yourself this question: What is the cost of continuing to put up with this? The risk to yourself is huge. The risk is accepting so much emotional abuse that you lose yourself entirely. You forget what's "normal" (healthy and acceptable) and what isn't. You forget what you want, what you value, and what you desire. Your needs get lost. You stop trusting yourself. Basically, you risk dissolving into a sad sucker, and nobody wants that.

Chapter 2

TRICKERY: UNMASKING THEIR GAMES

*"I just checked my receipt, and as it turns out,
I didn't buy any of your bullshit."*

IT WAS HER WEDDING DAY ON THE BEACH IN MEXICO, and all the bride wanted was no family drama and maybe even fun at her destination wedding. The bride was young and attractive and surrounded by many adoring friends and family who had come to celebrate. During the main course, her still-single older sister grabbed the microphone and spontaneously erupted into an unplanned speech. Wearing a big smile and a skintight dress, she told stories about the bride that made her sound like a bundle of problems before the groom came along and rescued her. While ignoring the uncomfortable silence and tense facial expressions in the room, the bride's sister gripped the microphone with purpose and laughed loudly at her own dull, inappropriate jokes. She peppered her speech with a few Spanish phrases for good measure. Finally, she concluded with how delighted she was that her little sister was marrying such a nice man! So now the family won't have to worry about her anymore! Isn't that sweet?

Egomaniacs won't flinch at snuffing out your flame to enhance their own image. This story about my client's sister demonstrates how insidious manipulation can be. What appears at first glance to be a big sister enthusiastically offering her blessing is actually an envious, attention-starved looney offering a backhanded compliment. When my client tried later to confront her sister about that speech, the sister insisted that it was a great speech. "Everyone loved it! People came up to me afterward and said it was hilarious! Maybe you didn't really get the jokes. Or maybe you're just too sensitive," she told my client. The only sounds of laughter detected on the video my client played for me was the punctuation of the speaker herself and maybe the muffled sound of one drunk guy in the far distance who was either laughing or having a seizure.

This one little tale is loaded with manipulation tactics. How many can you identify in this story? The rest of this chapter provides brief summaries of many of the most common manipulation tactics to help you get familiar with the terms that will be discussed in this book. When you get to the end of the list, reread the wedding story and count how many manipulation tactics Bridesmaid-zilla used.

Manipulation Tactics 101

The manipulation tactics described in the following are meant for you to identify and label the tactics that might be used on you by an egomaniac. Understanding these tactics will help you recognize what might be happening to you. These terms will be referenced throughout the book, and you can refer to this chapter while reading—it serves as sort of a glossary.

CONTROL

This book has an entire chapter on Control Freaks for a reason. Control exists in many forms, ranging from extreme and overt control to the quietly punishing kind. My client's girlfriend told him to stop listening to certain podcasts and news channels because she didn't agree with their politics. This wasn't a mere suggestion. When he insisted that he wanted to hear what the other side had to say, she became furious and accused him of disrespecting her. This is overt control. More subtle varieties of control are featured in some of the other tactics described in the following, such as intimidation, emotional blackmail, and more.

Overly possessive behavior is also a form of control. When people sabotage your friendships, trash talk your best friends, and try to limit your time with other people, they are deliberately shrinking your social network so you have fewer places to turn once you're sick of their shit. It's also a great way to prevent you from talking to someone else about his latest asshole stunt, so that your ball-busting, giving-zero-fucks, and ready-to-kick-down-doors-to-save-you-from-a-bad-guy best friend doesn't hear your story and go, "No, this one is bad news. Dump him immediately."

INTIMIDATION

Some manipulators make threats to arouse fear by inventing tragic consequences that will ensue if you don't do what they want. It's like emotional blackmail but louder. The ones with hot tempers might raise their voice with a sharp tone, scream at you, or verbally rip you to shreds. Others might harp relentlessly on one thing they want and beat you into submission with accusations about how stupid or selfish you're being. They might use guilt, tears, long emails, harsh text messages, any kind of crisis they can create, or fear they can arouse until you finally give up and give in to their demands.

BELITTLING

Narcissists tend to belittle other people. They present as arrogant and seem to have a superiority complex, but the arrogant façade is masking their fragile feelings of worthlessness. Their arrogant, superior attitude is like a barrier shielding others from the stink of their imperfections. The only way for them to feel superior is to make others feel inferior, which is why they demean and diminish others. Putting you down isn't necessarily meant to make you feel bad; it's more meant to make them feel good—it just happens to be at your expense. Just like in the wedding speech story, big sister was feeling insecure about her little sister getting married before her, so she portrayed her little sister as a basket case so she could feel better about herself.

In some cases, belittling is a subtle control tactic designed to whittle you down so when your self-esteem is in the toilet, you come to rely on your abuser for validation and direction.

BREADCRUMBING

Breadcrumbing is a pattern of inconsistent behavior manipulators use to keep their romantic victims attracted, confused, and guessing. They flirt without intention or follow-through. They give mixed signals galore. This is common among womanizers (see chapter 8) who enjoy the pursuit more than the actual relationship. People who breadcrumb are unpredictable and erratic and give you just enough crumbs to keep you coming back for more. There are many possible explanations for why they string you along with crumbs. Maybe they don't want a real commitment or anything serious, but they still want to be able to see you (and several others) here and there. Maybe they met someone else they like more but also don't want to burn a bridge, so they keep you waiting in the wings in case it doesn't work out with their new flavor of the month. The possibilities here are endless.

GASLIGHTING

Manipulators will tell you that what you saw, heard, or experienced did not actually happen. They deny what happened so explicitly and resolutely that they make you question your own reality. When Brides-maid-zilla, who gave a rotten speech, denied there was anything wrong with it and even insisted the crowd loved it, she was gaslighting her sister. It's as mind-boggling as catching a dumb kid with his hand in the cookie jar and crumbs all over his face as he swears that he hasn't been eating the cookies. Except this is not a dumb kid. It might be as daring and brazen as one, but the gaslighter plays a mind game that tests your sanity. "Are you crazy?" they might accuse you when you confront them, and they do it in such a way that you wonder whether you are actually going crazy. They might cast you as a mental patient who sees things that aren't there. They might cast a reliable witness as a full-blown liar. They rewrite history for you, enslaving you to their version of reality.

PROJECTION

Projection is like gaslighting, but it is more specific in the way that it redirects blame back on the victim. The projectionist simply flips the blame around. It's a thief accusing you of being greedy, an unfaithful spouse accusing you of cheating, an alcoholic accusing you of drinking too much. This tactic is about getting you to believe once and for all that they are right; you are the problem, not them. You are the crazy one, the greedy one, the dishonest one, the selfish one, the villain, the ultimate fuckup, not them.

PLAYING THE VICTIM

While victimizing oneself might sound counterintuitive to the arro-gance of a narcissistic hothead who's trying to trick you, playing the victim means you (or whoever their opponent in this drama is) must be the villain. The victim role allows them to escape responsibility for their actions, and they get the added bonus of guilting you with all the pity and sympathy they've aroused. They stockpile complaints to break you down and make you feel remorse so that hopefully by the end of their sad-sack diatribe, you start thinking, *Wow, I've done so many terrible things to this innocent person who is now so angry with me!* They want you to feel so sorry for them that you will do whatever it takes to earn back their affection. They go overboard and become overly dramatic as they express the unfairness of it all! The victim has many different masks: the pout, the sulk, the frown, the rage, the silent treatment, the fake tears in front of you as well as the fake tears when talking about you behind your back.

MARTYRDOM

Similar to playing the victim is the martyr tactic, which is a sad song that goes, "Look at everything I do for you, and I get nothing in return." When someone says, ". . . after all I've done for you," they are letting you know that what they did was transactional. They are urging you to step up your game in your efforts to make them happy and fulfill their demands. Often those things that they "do for you" are not things you ever asked for or wanted them to do in the first place. Maybe you did not want them to intrude the way they did under the context of "helping you," but that becomes hard to explain in the moment when they are accusing you of being ungrateful. The timing then becomes perfect for them to artfully position themselves to say, "If you don't do this for me now, I'm never doing anything for you ever again." It's a guilt trip, and the destination is, "Now give me whatever the hell I want." Good times.

WORD SALAD

Manipulators are skilled at using convoluted language to dodge questions and shirk responsibility. They might use big words, obscure terminology, and technical language to keep you confused. When my client asked his brother about the large sum of money he had contributed to make repairs on the vacation home they own together, which had been delayed for two years, he fired back an incoherent word salad. Sounding like a civil engineer all of a sudden, he rattled off something about *contractors and the hydraulic system under the ground and the city issuing a license that takes months and months but don't worry I'm friends with the mayor, and the architectural engineer declared a special tax incentive for eco-friendly installations combined with plumbing, firewalls, and fiber optic networks but the wire transfer is still pending so we have to wait and after that we can start.* Um okay, wait, what? Who wants to even try to understand this, let alone argue with it.

STONEWALLING

Stonewalling is a tactic to dodge confrontation by shutting the other person out. This is a more passive, subtle way of diminishing you and stripping you of your power. This usually happens when they get caught mid-stunt. They don't have a cover-up or a way out. For once, they are speechless; they are not going to admit to what they did. This is when they go radio silent or disappear. The last thing they want to do is talk about what they know they did, now that they know you know. They might say they need to step back from the relationship, and if they live with you and can't do that, then they might just ignore you, making you squirm in discomfort. Either way, they have a banana in their ear, and they aren't taking it out.

EMOTIONAL BLACKMAIL

This manipulation uses threats and punishment, directly or indirectly, to get compliance. They might threaten to end the relationship or to harm themselves, or they become so depressed and sad without you or what they want in that moment (*wahhhh!*) that you feel it's easier to just give in to their demands. Emotional blackmailers always want more, no matter how much you give them. It's an endless well of needs that you will never fill. Emotional blackmailers often make promises they don't keep. They completely ignore your needs. They boldly label you "selfish" or "lazy" or "ice cold" when you don't respond to their demands.

GUILT AND PUNISHMENT

Once the abuser successfully guilts and shames you, they have perfectly positioned themselves to slap on a self-serving punishment as a way to control you. It sounds like this: "You've done this terrible thing, so now you are going to have to do what I want, to prove that you really love me and are deserving of me." A famous sex cult leader named Keith Raniere locked a young woman in a solitary room for two whole years because she "disrespected" Mr. Horny Pants by kissing another guy, someone she actually liked. More tales to come on that sicko in chapter 5.

PRIZE DANGLING

You might have heard the sales and marketing term "bait and switch," which is when you are promised a deal that sounds too good to be true because it is actually a ploy to pull you in and get you to make even pricier purchases. Prize dangling is similar in the sense that the egomaniac dangles something in front of you that they know you want, but they don't uphold their end of the bargain. Another term for the same idea is "future faking." Once manipulators have learned about your weaknesses, they lure you in with false promises. They make promises and dangle prizes to win your loyalty, affection, and cooperation. They might ask for a favor, promising you something valuable in return, but then never deliver what they promised. It can be as simple as, "If you loan me a thousand dollars, I'll be able to pay you back triple what you gave me!" The Bad Vegan con artist did this when he insisted that his girlfriend continue to give him hundreds of thousands of dollars so she could obtain millions more and live in a special universe where her dog would become immortal. This is a true story, believe it or not.

THE DOUBLE BIND

The double bind is a conflicting message that keeps you stuck. It's when you are confronted with two undesirable options, rendering you hopeless. This is how your manipulator keeps you weak because you can't win no matter which course of action you choose. For example, you are told that you should be honest and stop being so agreeable, yet when you speak your mind, you are chewed up and spit out, cruelly put right back in your place. Another example is when your bitchy Martha Stewart–like incredible host of a wife bakes brownies for the whole family after telling you that you are overweight and should go on a diet. *Great, I'm going to enjoy them so much now, thanks.*

COGNITIVE EMPATHY

Cognitive empathy is a psychology term for fake concern when your manipulator pretends to care about your feelings in order to manipulate you. Bridesmaid-zilla pretended to care about her little sister's happiness on her wedding day in her patronizing speech as she served her signature, candy-coated venom to the audience. Backhanded compliments, like Bridesmaid-zilla's speech, are a form of cognitive empathy.

Manipulators, skilled at fishing for information, also wear a fake-concerned or caring expression while they are pulling information out of you to use against you or someone else later. This is just the foundation for the next tactic, operating your trigger buttons.

TRIGGER BUTTONS

Pushing your trigger buttons to provoke a reaction is a way to keep you feeling weak, guilty, or so messed up that you think nobody else will ever want you. Successfully convincing you that you're such a hot mess nobody would ever want you means you're not going anywhere. They trick you into confiding in them with cognitive empathy. After you've spilled personal information, the next time you have a fight, your own secrets, feelings, and trusted information will be hurled at you like psychological ammunition. "No wonder you got bullied in high school" or "Now I know why your ex-girlfriend left you." This is how they try to hold you captive in their psychological dungeon. If you believe their bullshit, it works.

FLYING MONKEYS

Flying monkeys is a term for those bamboozled little messenger people that manipulators always seem to keep in their wings. Once the manipulator gets the buy-in from their flying monkeys, these followers faithfully carry out the manipulator's message no matter how false, irrational, or crazy it might be. Manipulators know that messages have more impact if more than one person says it, and most especially when it comes from someone else, particularly when it is *about* them. Flying monkeys are enablers who cannot see any wrongdoing in this person (the manipulator). Maybe it's their golden child, the leader they elected, or a con artist they have fallen head over heels for. Basically, this person is flawless in their eyes. This person could rob a bank right in front of them and they would still rationalize it somehow. It's like they are under a spell. You see this in cults. A woman in Idaho was convicted of murdering her own children while allegedly under a spell like this.

SMEAR CAMPAIGNS

Some manipulators are vindictive. Smear campaigns are the unfortunate result of getting on the bad side of someone like this. If narcissistic-oriented individuals feel threatened enough by you, they might attempt to destroy your reputation and other relationships. This could be someone you've offended who is getting back at you, or someone you embarrassed or outshone in some way who wants to tear you down. It could be a political opponent or anyone who feels you are a threat to their image as a flawless, miraculous, shining star. The smear campaigner could be the golden child at home or a bully at school who feels you are catching up to their greatness, so they create denigrating rumors about you. Political candidates do this when they try to win elections by accusing their opponents of behaviors like sexual harassment and eating babies in basements.

TRIANGULATION

When narcissists and master manipulators feel unsuccessful in their attempts to control you, they might turn to more sophisticated manipulation tactics like triangulation in which they use other people to control communication between parties and strengthen their position over you. Here are some of the ways a manipulator might do this:

- **Using Flying Monkeys**—Bringing other people in to deliver their messages and warnings so that their opinion or position appears more popular or acceptable. (See flying monkeys from earlier.)

- **Fabricating a Consensus**—Manipulators try to tip the scales in their favor in an argument by misquoting a third party or appealing to authority. "Everyone I've asked agrees with me on this issue." (Reality: I pretended to take a poll, so you'll be convinced I'm right and you're wrong.) Or, "Mom thinks I'm a better host than you, which is why Thanksgiving will be at my house again this year." (Reality: I want to host Thanksgiving every year, so I'll just pretend that's what everyone else wants too.) Or, "All our cousins think your new boyfriend is a loser." (Reality: I think your new boyfriend is a loser, and maybe you'll believe he's a loser if our entire family thinks he's one too.)

- **Gathering Allies**—When they complain to another relative, mutual friend, or coworker about the other person, they are not just venting or confiding in their soul mates; they are priming them to take their side and forming their army. Manipulative parents sometimes do this to their children. "Your mother is out of control. She has been yelling at me all day. You need to tell her to calm down."

- **Splitting**—Divide and conquer tactics of turning people against each other to manipulate both sides. The manipulator engineers a rivalry between two people and keeps them from communicating with each other so the mustache-twirling evil-plotter can control what each person believes. Turning the two against each other is meant to result in increased trust and favor toward the manipulator. Since manipulators prey on the weaknesses of people, they look for a small rift or tragic event to drive a deeper wedge between these parties. Breakups, divorces, funerals, economic recessions, and pandemics are fruitful opportunities for the divide-and-conquer scheme. For example, the narcissistic golden child still wants Mommy and Daddy all to herself, but now that her sister just got into Harvard, she tells her, "Mom and Dad never thought you'd pull off getting into an Ivy League school, but I always knew you could." (That statement is also a backhanded compliment, but it's meant to create tension between her sister and her parents.) Next, Bitter Sister turns to Mom and Dad to privately announce, "I'm so proud of her. Too bad she doesn't recognize everything you two have done to support her." If the parents are dumb enough to buy into this crap, they might decide to spend all their extra cash on Bitter Sister and let the "ungrateful" Harvard student fend for herself. This is Bitter Sister's greedy attempt to hoard all the resources for herself and not have to share with her sibling.

You might be reading some of these anecdotes while thinking, *Wait, I know someone who has done this to me once,* or even, *I think I might have done one of these things before.* These tactics are defense mechanisms as well as manipulation tactics. This means they are unhealthy ways to cope with distress or conflict. If someone has done something like this once or twice, it's not gold star behavior, but it doesn't necessarily mean they are a narcissist or master manipulator. If it's a pattern that continues to repeat, however, I recommend that you beware.

Deconstructing Bridesmaid-zilla's Speech

Manipulators don't stop at one tactic; they rely on a myriad of tactics at once. They keep pulling tricks out of an endless sleeve until they get their point across or get what they want. Think of how many tactics Bridesmaid-zilla used in her speech once she had a captive audience. How many did you count? (1) As mentioned, she delivered a bold, backhanded compliment while pretending to care about her little sister (cognitive empathy). (2) She publicly belittled her. (3) You might say her belittling narrative was also a form of projection, as she tried to cast her sister as a hopeless loser before the groom came along, when in reality she probably felt deep down like the loser as the older sister, still single, with no suitors in sight. (4) She relied on gaslighting to dismiss her sister's feelings about her rude speech, claiming the bride didn't get her jokes and she's too sensitive. (5) Finally, it might not be a stretch to suggest that Bridesmaid-zilla's speech was a smear campaign, as she used the spotlight and captive audience to demean her sister and convince guests that the charming one to take notice of that evening was her, not the bride. Maybe you know someone like Bridesmaid-zilla—an attention-seeking egomaniac who is willing to trash you or anyone else to maintain her position as the fairest of them all.

The chapters in part 2 illustrate the types of people you might encounter who use these manipulation tactics. These archetypes are meant to help you recognize your specific manipulator so you can deepen your understanding of what is driving their behavior and how you can more effectively manage them. Each one includes a short list of their preferred manipulation tactics, how they use them on you, and pro tips on ways to deal with them.

PART TWO

Know Your
Enemy

Chapter 3

THE EGOMANIAC

A look behind the mask of grandiosity: deep, suppressed shame
Tactics used: belittling, gaslighting, projection,
smear campaign, triangulation

LET'S START WITH THE CORE TRAIT of your standard asshole, narcissist, or master manipulator: ego. They all have massive, fragile egos. Whether they are a drama queen who loves to play the victim, a control freak who executes heavy-handed power and control, a bully who terrorizes people for sport, a pathological liar who cheats and steals, or a womanizer who callously preys on vulnerable women, at the core of it all, they are all extremely egocentric. They are obsessed with themselves in a way that minimizes and devalues other people. This chapter on Egomaniacs can be seen as the umbrella chapter for all the other chapters in this section because they are all essentially Egomaniacs. The other ones are just special kinds of Egomaniacs.

I knew a guy once named Billy. Billy the Grandstander. Billy grew up in an upper-middle class family but liked to make believe that they were royals of some sort. He would talk about his noble grandparents to just about anyone who would listen. When you would meet Billy for the first time, the first thing he would do is talk about himself as if he were reading you his resume: "Hi, I'm Billy, an actor, writer, producer, singer, songwriter, dancer, director, and artist extraordinaire!" Billy was consistently unemployed, yet he always talked about his latest professional dibblings and dabblings with great enthusiasm. He was always either up for the next award-winning acting role, hired to write a groundbreaking story, or launching a start-up company that was currently rounding up investors. Regardless of the occasion, he dressed with pizzazz, dripping in hair gel and Swiss watches. He barely listened to a word anyone else had to say, as he was on stage every moment of his life.

Like most Egomaniacs, Billy is self-entitled, which means he feels that he should get cash and prizes without having to actually earn them or work for them. Instead of getting a regular job, he "borrowed" money from his parents and their generous friends—he convinced all of them that they were supporting his next big creative idea. If only Italian-made shoes, expensive restaurant bills, and trips to Europe were an "idea."

Egomaniacs are so obsessed with feeling good about themselves that they manage to delude themselves into believing their own fictional storytelling about their greatness. They believe their own bullshit because, unlike healthy, well-adjusted people, they *need* to believe their bullshit in order to survive. The grandiosity, magical thinking, and self-aggrandizing narrative shields them from their deeply suppressed shame. We all feel some level of shame from time to time, but Egomaniacs design their entire lives around avoiding any connection to their shame. High levels of narcissism do not allow any dose of uncomfortable reality to seep in. The way they see it, they are either exceptional or they are nothing. For people like this, there is no in-between, so the only way to reconcile the ugly truth of their own flawed selves is magical thinking. They actually believe they are entertaining the crowd despite many frowns, eye rolls, and awkward silences (think back to Bridesmaid-zilla's speech at the wedding). They truly believe they have accomplished a lot when they have, in reality, accomplished mostly financial debt and the disappointment of other people.

You might be wondering what the harm is with someone like Billy. He sounds like fun! True, Billy can be fun. He can be a riot, actually. But what happens when you get too close to someone like Billy? Here's what can happen. You might be one of the friends, neighbors, aunts, uncles, or cousins who loans Billy a large chunk of money you'll never see again. You might be someone he feels entitled to ask a favor from, and maybe he goes batshit crazy when you say no to requests like bringing him to an intimate party he's not invited to or letting him borrow your brand-new dirt bike, not to mention a pile of cash you know you'll never see again. Also, keep in mind, while he is gossiping and complaining to you about all those other "losers", don't think he isn't also gossiping about you to them when you aren't around.

If you are already closely involved with a delusional Egomaniac, you don't need me to tell you what an emotional drain they become over time. They don't listen to your experience or your side of the story ever. They are always "right" and everybody else is wrong . . . or stupid. They constantly criticize you and put you down. Belittling you is their way of making you think twice before you open your mouth again to disagree. They gaslight you, leaving you confused about what you saw, heard, or know to be true. They might tell you everyone agrees with them and that you should be lucky to be with them. Their defenses are successful in somehow reducing you to a hot mess for feeling so emotional about the way you are being treated.

When big-time Egomaniacs are called out, they might turn the tables on you with lightning speed (projection). They might even disappear, drop you, or give you the silent treatment (stonewalling) because that harsh light of reality you shine on them is too hard for their fragile egos to bear. Their deep, untouchable shame prevents them from being able to handle the tiniest shred of criticism. This makes it difficult, perhaps impossible, for you to explain that they might have done something that bothers you. Communicating about their mis-deeds doesn't work because they are flawless human beings, remember?

I haven't seen Billy in years. He cut me out of his life when I asked him why he couldn't get a job before he would ask me for money. He rattled off an elaborate word salad explanation about why that was impossible and insisted that "everybody else trusts him with money" so clearly the problem here was me. Okay, *byeeeee.*

Egomaniacs like to be around people who fawn all over them in admiration. If anyone criticizes them or knocks them off their pedestal, they defame that person's character, drop that person like a hot potato, or perhaps both. Basically, it becomes really hard to exist as your own person, take a stand, or even take up any space around people like this.

So, what do you do around someone like this? You don't want to pump their ego any more than you want to ruffle their feathers. What are your options? The answer is bland indifference.

Think Like the Swiss

The country of Switzerland is famous for mastering the art of neutrality, and you might want to learn to do the same. Remain neither impressed nor critical. Resist the urge to argue, prove them wrong, or challenge their distortions and discrepancies. Remember, they designed their delusional defense mechanism out of survival. It's a bulletproof fortress against any information that challenges their way of thinking. Attempting to introduce reality or deconstruct their fairy tale with common sense is like tampering with a system that explodes when it detects a crack. Don't get involved in what goes on in their disturbed heads. Instead, protect your own fortress. You stay sane and safe when you know what's true, and you don't need to prove it to them or anyone else. Don't let the Egomaniac rattle you with false facts and outrageous accusations.

The Different Brands of Egomaniacs

Egomaniacs come in many varieties. Some are merely boasting and bragging relentlessly like the Showboater, which is relatively harmless, albeit annoying as hell. The more menacing ones are trying to run your life, like the Know-it-all, or trying to diminish you like the Minimizer. The following are some examples of specific types of Egomaniacs you might encounter with pro tips on how to handle each one.

THE SHOWBOATER

The Showboater, otherwise known as the show-off, the actor, the braggart, or the attention hog, is addicted to your applause, which is where they seek your affirmation and approval. They want to be admired by and even envied by others because deep down they feel an emptiness that can only be filled by the admiration of others. Impressing other people allows them to satisfy their urge for validation and extinguish their hidden shame for a fleeting moment. If it feels like they aren't listening much to you or anyone else, that's because they aren't. They have little interest in anyone else apart from the praise and validation others have to offer. *Enough about me, let's talk about you . . . what do you think of me?* That ancient joke will never die because there will always be people it skewers.

When they are dominating the conversation, bragging, and exaggerating (or even lying outright), just give the Showboater all the airtime they want and let them figuratively hang themselves. If nobody is competing with them for attention, eventually they'll sound like the self-absorbed drone that they are, and they wind up embarrassing themselves with nobody's help. Just nod along. Occasionally, you can blandly interject phrases like: *Is that so? Amazing. Good for you.*

THE UPSTAGER

You know the one. The person who always has an even better story to top yours every single time you share. They are basically the Showboater in competition with you and everyone else. Everything is a competition for this type of Egomaniac. The way they see it, when your stock goes up, theirs must go down, so they work tirelessly at always maintaining their number-one position. Your expression of pride or accomplishment pokes a giant hole in their ego balloon, so they pump themselves right back up by diminishing or demeaning you. Their insensitive comments are not necessarily aimed at hurting you; their purpose is to remove the shame of their real or imagined inferiority. Avoid taking this personally, and recognize the small child inside who is desperately seeking his turn for attention and praise.

A friend of mine who's a black belt instructor of martial arts was sharing a story about how he made his mugger think twice about robbing him when his dopey, overweight brother interrupts to announce that he would have just kicked him in the balls. Everyone laughed when he responded nonchalantly with, "Oh, sounds like you would have handled that situation so much better. Thank goodness you are here." Use that kind of sarcasm playfully and with caution. If they are not stable enough to handle a dose of sarcasm like that, then you can respond as you would to the Showboater, with complete indifference.

The need to upstage doesn't even have to be based on a prideful or positive situation; Egomaniacs are also happy to be the one who got it worse just so they can hog the spotlight as an even bigger victim than you. *You think your cavity is bad? Try getting a root canal!* Um, okay, I'll try that, thanks.

If it's a competition to gather the most attention, whether it's pity or praise, think for a moment about your willingness to participate in such a nonsense competition. Who needs to win that competition?

If they do, it's because their ego counts on it for survival. That is their oxygen. Think of it this way: letting them win that silly competition is a way for you to recognize your own inner strength by not counting on the external environment to feel good about yourself. *Okay, you win, congratulations, do you want a sticker?* Probably best not to say that out loud, but you can think it to yourself if it helps you smile confidently without breaking your composure.

THE KNOW-IT-ALL

Some situations call for the subject matter experts with degrees and credentials who love to share what they know without worrying about whether they sound arrogant or not. That's not what I'm talking about. I'm referring, instead, to the ignorant, snide talker with a superiority complex who is not capable of taking in new information. For this person, listening to anyone else confirms that he is not superior (uh-oh!) and is, therefore, inferior to whomever he hands over the microphone and podium. So instead of listening and validating someone else's point of view, he strategizes to remain the authority on the topic at hand. His strategy is to essentially double down on squashing the spirit of his perceived opponent.

Always remember to pick your battles wisely, especially when dealing with a Know-it-all. When they are arguing with you and insisting they are right and you are wrong, do not get sucked into an argument you can't win. Stop to consider whether you need to win that argument. If it's not important, let it go. For example, let's say you're a happy, healthy vegan. Do you really need to convince your carnivore twerp uncle that you're getting enough protein from beans and legumes? Let him enjoy his cheeseburgers and believe that you will probably wilt away from malnutrition. You will prove him wrong when you don't wilt away and remain healthy. That should be enough.

If you know what the truth is, let that be enough for you. Remember to stay out of their heads. The six inches between their two ears is none of your business, and whatever is going on in there is not your job to fix. When you retire from the mission of changing how they think, not only is it a huge relief but it's also how you stay sane. Staying out of their crazy head is how you protect your fortress.

You might use these responses:

- We just don't see it the same way, and that's okay.

- Let's just agree to disagree.

- I understand what you are saying; my perspective is very different.

- Thank you for sharing your unique point of view.

- Okay, I accept that that's how you see things. I don't like it, but I accept it.

- You've given me some interesting things to think about. (You can think about it, but it doesn't mean you will change your mind.)

THE MINIMIZER

In an argument, the Egomaniac doesn't want to hear about your feelings. The way they see it, validating your feelings makes you more important than them, even for a tiny moment. Or worse yet, what if anything you say involves the truth about their behavior, a reality they work hard at twisting, distorting, or outright denying? They would rather minimize your experience than give it any airtime or validation. They do that with comments meant to minimize and diminish your experience, such as, "Oh come on, it wasn't that bad" or "Can't you take a joke?"

Don't work up a sweat trying to defend, explain, or prove yourself. Remain unflappable as you hold them accountable for their own words. Repeat what they've said back to them or ask them to elaborate more on what they've said so the tactics they use to drown you out are more obvious. Resist the urge to continue to argue your point. You might use these responses:

- What do you mean by that?
- You're right, I didn't get your joke; can you explain why that's supposed to be funny?
- You really don't understand why it's a big deal?
- I'll let you think about what you said/did on your own time since we don't seem to be getting anywhere in this conversation.

If you are dealing with a narcissist, you are better off disengaging entirely, rather than fighting to be heard or validated. Circular arguments are one of their favorite pastimes. All they want is for you to step into the ring with them while they blast you with manipulation tactics. Never allow yourself to get sucked into the temptation of defending yourself or trying to explain yourself to a narcissist. By engaging with them, you are giving them more words and ideas to use against you like ammunition. The more you argue your point, the more opportunity they have to flip the script, gaslight you, or take the argument in another direction. Sometimes the biggest power move of all is your silence.

Remember this:

You don't need to attend every argument you've been invited to.

Chapter 4

THE DRAMA QUEEN

A look behind the mask of the perpetual victim: fear of neglect or abandonment

Tactics used: playing the victim, martyrdom, emotional blackmail, guilt and punishment, trigger buttons, smear campaigns, triangulation

THE DRAMA QUEEN IS SO UNIVERSAL and ever present that society has even given her a name. Her name is Karen. It's the name given to self-entitled individuals who believe the rules don't apply to them—and then they promptly melt down when called out for their rude, self-absorbed, and outrageous behavior. We all know a Karen, and if we are blessed enough not to have a Karen at home, at work, at school, or in our social network, chances are we have seen a Karen captured on video somewhere on the internet. There is the Karen at the grocery store running amok and screaming her lungs out because the mask mandate is being enforced on her during the pandemic. There is the racist Karen at the park who becomes overly dramatic when a man politely asks her to leash her dog; she frantically calls the police to report that a Black man is harassing her. There is the Karen at Walmart, smashing candles in some sort of verbal protest against the Black Lives Matter movement. The list of Karen enactments is endless.

What sets Drama Queens apart from other types of manipulators is the way they play the victim to escape accountability. Like Egomaniacs, they need to feel special and important. Drama Queens, specifically, fear they won't be loved unless they are special and important. This fear of rejection is fed by their obsession with constant attention and their frantic fear of abandonment. They pose as victims to keep people invested in them. They do this several different ways. Drama Queens, although most often female, can be male or female, with many variations.

The Diva

The Diva is a self-entitled "star." The Diva believes in receiving special treatment due to her specialness and then melts down or raises hell when she doesn't get it. Certain celebrities are known for being Divas. They are the high-maintenance, difficult-to-work-with stars who have odd demands, like maybe they absolutely must have their special oat-milk matcha with a hint of turmeric over extra hot foam, or they must travel in an entourage with a million people who do nothing but sit around and make them feel amazing. Divas don't have to be famous; anyone who deems themselves important enough to insist that others scramble around to please them falls under the Diva category. If you are dealing with someone like this, stop tripping over yourself to please them. Part 3 of this book will help you recognize when you are overextending yourself to please this type of manipulator.

The Energy Vampire

The Energy Vampire is an attention-starved emotional parasite who sucks all the energy and empathy out of the room. They are often spotlight hogs with "Look at me!" engraved on their foreheads. The Energy Vampire, like the Diva, needs to be the center of attention. More specifically, Energy Vampires try to suck you into some kind of problem or tragedy. They vent relentlessly. They tell stories in which they star as the helpless victim, with zero interest in advice or solutions. Their tales of victimhood leave you utterly drained.

Have you ever hung out with someone and, no matter what is going on, that person constantly seems to be saying, "Let's get back to me!"? If your iPhone battery dies on your flaming hot ear every time they call you, you've got yourself an Energy Vampire.

How do you deal with this person before your energy supply is depleted? With Energy Vampires and Divas, limiting your exposure to doses you can tolerate can be helpful, as well as clarifying your availability up front. For example, let them know how many minutes you can spare on the phone before you have to hang up to get to something else. When the time is up, don't be afraid to interrupt and remind them you need to go. The pre-warning helps them absorb the shock of abrupt abandonment.

When you are forced to be physically in the same space with Divas and Energy Vampires, you can reduce your exposure by using buffers. Stick to larger groups—the larger the better—and bring a plus-one whenever possible. An extraverted plus-one who will do their share of the talking is even better, particularly when you're forced to sit down at the same table with the Energy Vampire. "The more the merrier" is almost always true, especially when it means more people to drown out the sound of an energy sucker.

When you find yourself pulled into an argument with Divas and Energy Vampires, stay calm and respond with noncombative firmness. Try not to get defensive or emotional while advocating for yourself. Stick to simple phrases that are noncombative to keep things from escalating, such as the following:

- That doesn't work for me.

- I understand how important that is for you, and I'm also telling you what is important for me.

- That's your choice to make (in response to an intimidation tactic or threat).

- Thanks for letting me know; I need to think all of that over.

- You've given me a lot to think about. Let me get back to you.

- I know you want a response now, but I need time to think about what you've said.

- I'd rather talk about this when things have calmed down. (I recommend using the word "things" or "we" rather than "you" to avoid blaming them.)

The idea here is to avoid the emotional roller coaster they are inviting you to ride with them. Stay grounded and calm. Stick to your convictions. If they get angry and hostile, disengage; you can let them get angry by themselves without your participation.

The Eternal Victim

The Eternal Victim is a self-pity party of one. They turn every conflict into a personal battle against themselves instead of examining their own role in conflicts, unfortunate events, or messes they might have created themselves. The Eternal Victim is the most blatant victim card user of them all. They manipulate you into believing they are not responsible for their problems so you will join them in blaming someone else. Unfortunately, sometimes that someone else is you.

A friend of mine had loaned her deadbeat brother a large sum of money. When she asked him about getting reimbursed many years later, his response to her was to stop harassing him. Classic victimization. News flash to deadbeat brother: the victim is the person waiting to get paid back by a selfish prick, not the person enjoying the reward of someone's generosity with zero accountability. Being held accountable for your own actions (borrowing money you have not returned) does not make you a victim, although Drama Queens, the masters of self-victimization, will try their best.

Eternal Victims might also be called Charming Victims since they are so skilled at painting a flawless, loveable portrait of themselves while casting everyone around them as villains. Did you see Hugh Grant's performance as a sociopathic murderer posing as a doting husband, a loving father, a caring doctor, and the most charismatic man ever on HBO's series *Undoing*? This psychological mystery thriller centered around his guilt or innocence regarding the heinous murder of the woman with whom he had an affair. This character was a brilliant portrayal of the Eternal Victim casting himself as a good man charged with murder when all he "really" did was have a regrettable affair. He plays the victim card so perfectly that it makes you want to ignore the mounting evidence and believe his distorted narrative that he is tragically caught in a horrific mess of circumstances. A handsome, charming, wealthy man just couldn't resist the fruit of a seductive young woman, and now he is accused of murder (gasp!). What an unfortunate twist of events! Except he *did* commit the murder.

The devil doesn't show up in red horns and a pitchfork announcing they are the devil. They are handsome devils, sexy devils, and most of all, they artfully convince you that they are not the villains in the story; they are the victims. They make an insidious mess and then cry a sad sob story when they are asked to take responsibility for their actions. They pull out all the stops to manipulate you into believing that they are not responsible for the messes they have created. They blame someone else, gaslight you, or give you the silent treatment for accusing them. They triangulate entire families and workplaces to convince you they are innocent.

My client Amber was married to a Charming Victim. Pat was one of those affable guys who made friends with everyone everywhere he went. Pat was the Mayor of Nowhere. Who doesn't love a guy like that? Except this guy completely ignored Amber at home. She worked full-time and raised their twin toddlers, while he barely lifted a finger to help. Taking work calls at night while looking after their screaming kids stressed her out. When she asked her oblivious husband to help, he would "watch" the kids while staring at half-naked girls on his phone. His idea of making them dinner was heating up those dinosaur-shaped chicken nuggets in the microwave and leaving them in front of the TV. On the weekends, he would often come home from the golf course smelling of beer and occasionally pass out on the living room floor before their twins were put to bed. A few times, he got up in the middle of the night after binge drinking all day and ate the kids' packed lunches in the fridge. When Amber questioned the lunch items that had vanished overnight, he played dumb and pretended that he did not wake up half drunk with acid belly and inhale everything in sight. Some good gaslighting right there. She had witnessed him getting out of bed at two in the morning to make his way to the kitchen where he rummaged around noisily; but sure, someone else must have broken into the house to eat the contents of the kids' lunchboxes and then quietly left undetected. That makes so much more sense, right?

This behavior enraged a stressed-out, overworked, and under-appreciated Amber, who was starting to lose her lid. At times, she erupted into a fit about how selfish and useless he was. Pat would tell their family and friends that Amber had a temper and was so mean to him. He would tell anyone who listened that all his attempts to help her at home were never good enough. He told a compelling story about a mean wife who wouldn't have sex with him anymore. As if a passed-out drunk, lazy fool snoozing on the sofa at bedtime is the least bit tempting to a hardworking mother of two. Amber eventually filed for divorce. The hardest part for Amber was learning how to stop reacting to him, even while he was making his case as a victim and distorting reality to her and everyone in their circle.

BULLSHIT ALERT

The best way to protect yourself from Eternal Victims or anyone playing the victim, is to notice when they are using the victim card and to avoid falling for it. Pay close attention to when this person avoids taking any responsibility for their own actions. Notice when they blame people around them instead of acknowledging their own role. When their stories are riddled with self-pity and all the blame is firing outward, you can be pretty sure they are playing the victim.

Do not get sucked into the vortex. Do not believe their tales of self-victimization and buy their bullshit. They are feeding you self-pity soup; it's nothing but a one-sided, distorted story about their plight, as a way to suck you into their drama and manipulate you. Arousing your pity is how they get what they want from you. They might want your money, your time, your attention, your energy, or to turn you against someone else and triangulate the heck out of you. Most often, they want you to rescue them in some fashion, and it's almost always something you will regret having done later. Whatever it is, you are not put on this planet to feed their wild ego so do not participate in the Drama Queen's psychodrama.

Of course, when you refuse to participate, they won't like it. You can prevent the situation from escalating by remaining calm with your own awareness of how they are trying to manipulate you into believing them, helping them, rescuing them, or any other form of buying their bullshit. Maybe now you're thinking, *Okay, yeah, easier said than done, how the hell do I do that?* Here are some tips to keep the situation from escalating:

- *First of all, stay calm*: Don't get sucked into the vortex with the Eternal Victim. Just because they get all crazy and don't remain calm doesn't mean you have to get crazy with them. Don't meet them at their level. Take deep breaths and focus on separating yourself from their drama. Sometimes it helps to imagine a glass gate closing between you so you can tuck yourself into your own imaginary bubble. Use any imagery that works for you to visually separate yourself from them. One of my clients lives on a farm, and she said she likes to imagine a beehive falling on her mother's head every time she yells at her. The buzzing sound of bumblebees soothes her.

- *Single-issue focus*: Stick to one issue at a time. If the Eternal Victim stockpiles complaints or branches out in a thousand different directions about everything you've ever done over the last ten years, don't scramble around with them trying to put out each individual fire. Don't get defensive. Redirect them back to the first thing they said and insist on discussing one issue at a time. Or in reverse, if they are catastrophizing and drawing overly dramatic conclusions in response to your criticism of them or one specific incident, do the same redirecting to a single issue at a time.

  Like this: (In response to hearing what they've done to upset you)—

  VICTIM: I must be a terrible mother (father/wife/husband/person)!

  YOU: We are talking about one isolated incident. Can we stay focused on that?

- *Reflecting back*: Simply repeat their own nonsense back to them so they can hear it. Drama Queens frequently make outrageous statements. When one comes out of their mouth and we hear their batshit-crazy babble, we tend to react to the insanity of it and then flip out ourselves. This quickly escalates the situation. Instead of flipping out and going, "WTF! Are you insane?!" just calmly repeat their crazy shit right back, like an echo. Give them a chance to hear how crazy their shit sounds. With any luck, they might try to backpedal and bring the intensity level down on their own.

Like this:

YOU: How did you lose your job?

VICTIM: I got fired because my boss hates me!

YOU: Your boss hates you?

Pause right there. Wait long enough for them to backpedal or explain what's actually going on.

The Martyr

The Martyr is a sad Control Freak with poor boundaries who plays the victim by doing everything for everyone but (sigh!) gets nothing in return. (Do you hear a violin playing in the background?)

Perpetually suffering, they like to tell embellished stories about their latest woe, usually involving a sacrifice they made for someone else or others who don't seem to appreciate all they've done. What they are actually doing through the use of these stories is constructing an image of themselves that appears to be altruistic or heroic. Like Control Freaks, they tend to invade your space and take over without asking your permission. Yes, they do tend to do a lot of things for other people, initiate and spearhead tasks on their own, and volunteer their time and energy to help. The problem is that Martyrs do this while expecting praise and special recognition. Or they are expecting something in return. Beyond that, they are doing things the recipients never asked for and maybe didn't want them to be doing in the first place. Martyrs desperately need to see themselves as helpful and heroic. Sometimes this is because they need to be needed, so they don't see their own value unless someone needs them. They don't, however, realize that they are usually perceived by those receiving their unsolicited "help" as invasive and domineering. They become emotionally unglued when people don't see them as they want to be seen. Rather than seeing the other person's experience of them, they defend their almighty position in martyrdom, casting everyone else as selfish or lazy, in the hopes that this lands them the attention and pity they so desperately crave.

How do you respond to Martyrs who refuse to see things any other way? You can use techniques similar to those used with the Eternal Victim, but in this case, it might be even more important to remember that their thoughts and feelings are their own. You are not responsible for the way they see things. Just because they say they feel taken for granted or neglected, that doesn't make you a selfish, lazy, or bad person. You can acknowledge that they feel that way without becoming responsible for their feelings.

Like this:

MARTYR: Do I have to do EVERYTHING myself?!

RESPONSE: It sounds like *you* think you do.

This hands responsibility for their own feelings right back to them without invalidating them. It also has the potential to open a potentially productive discussion—if this person is capable of being rational. If so, invite the Martyr to share why she thinks this is the case, that she has to do everything herself. Remain single-issue focused by asking for one example at a time.

MARTYR: You don't appreciate anything I do for you!

RESPONSE: I'm happy to speak for myself. Which thing are you referring to?

Single-issue focus—if they start to stockpile several things, insist on discussing one example at a time.

The Dictator

The Dictator is a Drama Queen who is calling the shots. Drama Queens, similar to Control Freaks (in chapter 5), can be domineering, but they go about it in a crafty, victimized way. Their self-entitlement convinces them that everyone should orbit around them and obey their wishes. These are the people who melt down like a snowman in the sun when you don't do what they want. They become overly emotional and cry crocodile tears to move you to join their selfish agenda. Don't get swayed by this. Instead of feeling called to duty, remind them of what their own choices are.

A college girl is crying to her divorced father on the phone: "But I don't want your girlfriend to move in because then when I visit you over the holidays, I'll have to hear her baby crying at night. I don't want to live with a baby!" She is the twenty-year-old daughter of my client Josh, who has been divorced from her mother for more than ten years. The woman who recently moved in with him is the first one he has truly fallen in love with and makes him happy after a string of disappointing relationships. Her two-and-a-half-year-old child was an infant in her arms when they met for the first time, and he cares for this child like his own. Josh has been working hard at learning to stop spoiling his daughter out of guilt over divorcing her mother.

Instead of succumbing to the temptation of accommodating her selfish demands or arguing about how unfair they are, he firmly, noncombatively sets his boundaries the way he has learned to. He simply redirects her own choices back to her. "Okay, well it sounds like your choices are either to not visit me or to visit me and accept the way my life is now. I'm very happy, and I hope you will still come over." That's it, no discussion about how a grown man will rearrange his life for his spoiled grown-up child.

When they insist you do what they want after you've said no, here are some sample phrases to try. It's important you state these calmly and firmly.

- I hear what you're saying. Still, my answer isn't going to change.

- Even if you can't understand my reasons, I need you to respect my decision.

- I know you don't like my decision, but it's not up for debate.

- You can say whatever you like about this matter and I will listen, but I'm not going to change my mind.

Whether you're dealing with a Diva, an Energy Vampire, an Eternal Victim, a Martyr or a Dictator, it all boils down to drama that you do not need in your life. They are playing the victim in the hopes that your kind nature will take pity on them, believe their twisted narrative and give them what they want. Don't fall for it. Stay away from this kind of energy and set firm boundaries.

Remember this:

When people around you are losing their heads, that's when it's most important for you to hold onto yours at all costs.

Chapter 5

THE CONTROL FREAK

A look behind the mask of power and control: fear of weakness
Tactics used: control, intimidation, emotional blackmail, guilt and
punishment, double bind, trigger buttons, belittling, triangulation

CAN YOU THINK OF ANYTHING MORE CONTROL FREAKISH than branding your very
own band of sex slaves? That is what convicted sex cult leader Keith
Raniere was doing before he was sentenced to 120 years of prison
in 2020 for sex trafficking, racketeering, fraud, and other crimes. In
case you don't remember or never heard of the infamous Hollywood
sex cult leader, he cofounded a multilevel marketing company called
NXIVM, a purported self-help business where young women were
housed, forced to follow near-starvation diets, blackmailed, groomed
to have sex with the horny sicko in charge, and branded with his
initials from a hot piece of metal over their vaginas. The high level
of manipulation tactics used on everyone involved in his powerful
scheme is astounding. He used extreme and overt control, of course,
but also intimidation, blackmail, guilt and punishment, prize dangling,
cognitive empathy, trigger buttons, gaslighting, and triangulation—and
that was probably just his warm-up routine. He's a master manipulator
at the highest level. Thousands of people joined his cult, including

celebrities, as he formed alliances with powerful, wealthy people all over the world.

The Control Freak ultimately fears losing control and consequently feeling weak and powerless. There are different reasons for this. Control issues can be complex. The analysis depends on the magnitude of control and what drives their urge to control.

In some cases, the urge to control is driven by a form of anxiety, usually Obsessive Compulsive Disorder, which tends to be a more innocuous and less toxic kind of control, as well as other types of anxiety. Anxiety is less about deliberate manipulation and more about managing fear: fear of the unknown, fear of the future, fear of rejection, fear of just about anything. The coping mechanism of these people is to latch on to control. They are often big planners (creating plans helps the Control Freak feel secure and regain a feeling of control). They are often big talkers who appear to want to rant and ramble endlessly, but usually their goal is to arrive at solutions. They might obsess, worry, harp on things, and have difficulty letting go. They tend to appear rigid because maybe they just want the towels folded a certain way or their coffee mug posing in a specific spot. If you are dealing with someone prone to anxiety, this behavior might be easier to work through if the person is willing to recognize their control issues and how they are impacting your relationship.

On the other hand, if their fear is driven by a narcissistic need to feel powerful, consider yourself in hotter water. This kind of person gets off on power and control. Their need to feel powerful is driven by their hidden, suppressed fear of feeling weak and powerless; essentially, they feel like they are not enough. They have a deep-seated need to control situations like the anxious controller, but also people. Controlling and manipulating other people feeds their ego. This is how they convince themselves they are important. Their need to feel important overrides everything and everyone at all times. This person will never recognize or admit to their attempts to control you or a situation. If this is the case, you are more likely dealing with a Control Freak with a capital C.

Control Freaks are often insanely possessive. Diminishing your social network is a way to have more influence and exert even more control. Sex Cult King Keith Raniere, for example, did that by containing everyone physically on his grounds, psychologically through his self-help program, and sexually as his branded slaves while creating an exclusive, esoteric network of followers who learned never to question him. They stopped associating with friends and family outside of their cult and willingly cut ties with friends and family who disapproved.

You can imagine how much easier it is to control your significant other when they're not out brunching with someone named Susan who listens to a full report on the latest dickhead maneuver and then says, "Yeah, no, you need to ditch this guy," while chewing lettuce and washing it down with bottomless mimosas. The last thing a Control Freak needs is you coming home with liquid courage and Susan's endorsement that he's bad news so you can start setting boundaries and threatening to break up with him. Let's keep you at home where you can't get validation from the outside world that his behavior is toxic, ridiculous, and not acceptable. It's essentially the same tactic used by kidnappers and sex traffickers who keep their victims trapped in a basement, only more subtle. It might sound like this, instead: "I don't want you spending too much time with Susan because she's an ultra-feminist man-hater." Statements like that are a great way to keep you guessing with perpetual self-doubt and a haze of madness: *Hmm, is Susan a man-hater, or does she just not approve of this particular man's behavior?* After a while you become so gaslit, it's hard to know what to think anymore.

Possessive Control Freaks do not just limit your access to close friends; sometimes they limit access to your family. This is because, naturally, the Control Freak doesn't want your supportive parents, brothers, sisters, uncles—or whoever—setting you straight and then helping you pack your bags to bounce the second he goes to the grocery store. They also most definitely restrict communication with other men and women as potential romantic prospects. If you're a heterosexual female, for example, you might not be able to have a normal conversation with a guy when the Control Freak is around. The same thing goes in reverse. If you're a heterosexual male, if you even look at another girl in front of her, you've unwittingly stepped into the battlefield of insanity. Control Freaks micromanage every move you make. In addition to controlling the people you are allowed to see, they might also control your communication through your devices by composing text messages for you or even demanding that you stop responding to certain people altogether. The most deceptive manipulators will go so far as to delete messages or block people from your phone without your knowledge. If you're dealing with someone this controlling, keep your devices and passwords safe and private, no matter what.

Control Freaks can be male or female. My clients have reported some batshit-crazy Control Freak examples, like my client Jay who was told he was not allowed to listen to podcasts that conflicted with his girlfriend's political ideology, insisting it "disrespected" her. I'll never forget the day Jay walked into my office. He was a hunky African American athlete who towered over me at somewhere between six and seven feet tall. At first glance, he looked like a guy you don't want to mess with. He sat down on the sofa and showed me scathing text messages from his girlfriend that went on for paragraphs. His phone was flooded with chat bubbles of vitriol. As I got to know him, he proved to be a kind character who would undoubtedly hesitate to swat a fly. Unfortunately, the man became riddled with anxiety and traumatized by a dejected, angry woman who wouldn't stop chewing him out. Control Freaks come in all forms, and they will attempt to control anyone who lets them, regardless of their gender, age, role, shape, or size.

Control Freaks use emotional blackmail, with their balls swinging so low it's hard to believe they are not the least bit concerned about their own transparency. Like when Keith Raniere's sex slaves were forced to turn over nude photos and reveal their darkest secrets for him to use as blackmail, ensuring their silence. Sex Kook Keith and his flying monkeys called it "collateral," as if that were any kind of disguise for the most classic of blackmail schemes.

More often, however, the blackmail is more subtle. The underlying message is essentially, *if you don't do what I want, I will make you suffer and pay*. Control Freaks prey on your sense of obligation, fear, or guilt, and they do this while concealing the pressure they're applying. They artfully operate your trigger buttons, often the ones they installed themselves, especially if this person is a family member. They know exactly which button to push to pressure you into submission. The call to duty might sound like this: "You're the *only one* who can help me." Or they might say, "If you leave me, I'll tell everyone how abusive you are," keeping you handcuffed to a nutcase in the hopes of avoiding a smear campaign.

Guilt and punishment happen when you dare to defy or disrespect the Control Freak. The punishment never fits the crime. Keith Raniere maintained a harem of women whom he regularly seduced, had sex with, and in some cases raped. One of his very young virgin slaves developed feelings for another guy in the cult and shared a kiss with him. King Sex Kook Keith felt so disrespected by this act that he punished her by locking her up in a small room where she remained isolated and was forced to poop and pee in a bucket for two years. Again, this is the extreme side of controlling with a capital C to the max.

To scale this down to people in toxic relationships instead of cults, let's talk about my client Stacy, who went on a business trip in the early stage of her career. A young, married business executive in her midtwenties, her eagerness to network sent her spiraling into an unexpected drinking spree that started at happy hour, continued throughout the evening, and landed her in the hotel room of another guy. They had drunken sex, an interlude she could barely remember. She then flew home, riddled with guilt. She immediately confessed to her husband what had happened. More than ten years after this singular incident occurred, her husband still enforces a rule that she be chaperoned on all future business trips. The last time she took a business trip, he insisted that her five-year-old son and the kid's grandma (yes, her mother-in-law!) join them. They turned out to be a huge distraction while she was trying to prove herself with her new coworkers, and shortly after, she was let go for strange reasons that were never made clear to her.

Control Freaks like to put you in a double bind, forcing you to choose between two undesirable options. Creating a panic of indecisiveness makes them feel more in control of you. The emotional dilemma that is "damned if you do, damned if you don't" is one of their favorite games because your emotional dilemma reinforces their control over you. When you plummet into an abyss of indecisiveness, they opportunistically rush in to decide for you.

At the root of every single tactic is the concept of trigger buttons. Understanding the victim's triggers or weaknesses is how a Control Freak breaks them down. Trigger buttons can be jealousy, resentment, or any weakness used against the victim. Planting seeds of self-doubt by belittling their victims in areas where they are already insecure whittles them down more and more until their self-esteem is in the toilet. At that point, the victim starts to rely on their manipulator for validation.

Control usually comes with criticism. When the criticism feels unfair and unrelenting, it could be designed to belittle the victim, which eventually beats them into submission. It eases the relationship into a master–servant dynamic if the victim falls for it. "Did I fix your meatloaf to your liking, sir?" You get the idea.

Control Freaks are masters at triangulation. They gather allies to assist them with enforcing control. Control Freak Keith Raniere indoctrinated thousands of people and turned them into an army of soldiers to help him enforce control. Anyone who falls out of line answers not only to the master manipulator in charge but also to his faithful followers and the flying monkeys who blindly serve him. The most manipulative Control Freak knows how and when to turn people against each other so the Control Freak can have each person all to himself, designing a form of loyalty that is served but not reciprocated. The Control Freak positions himself at the top corner of a triangle, so the other two corners serve him. He never serves the other two, and he controls and restricts the communication of the others.

For example, when the poor girl in the sex cult was held captive in a room for two years, Keith had convinced the other members that she was being punished and had to learn an important lesson. Nobody questioned him, and most importantly, nobody had access to her. The person chosen to slide food under her door was a woman who had already been primed to be jealous of her, so there was no risk of the two of them colluding. That right there is the art of control. The Control Freak understands that orchestrating jealousy or resentment between parties will keep them working for him, serving him, advocating for him, and carrying out all his wishes—but not helping each other.

Triangulation is most successful when the manipulator knows the victim's trigger buttons. Creating jealousy between two parties can form a triangle, naturally, but the possibilities are endless and sometimes less obvious than the aforementioned toxic love triangle. You might see this in families when parents who are getting divorced triangulate their child. This can take various forms: "Look, your mother is angry again, I guess she'll never be satisfied" or "Your father is never around when we need him." It's the basic idea of making an enemy out of the other parent to make the child favor the manipulative parent instead. These comments are like seeds the manipulator plants so over time they grow into the victim's own belief system. If you are the one in your family or social circle feeling caught in the middle, be sure to state that you refuse to get embroiled in their situation. Encourage them to work it out on their own.

You might say, "I hear you, but I can't get in the middle of this. You two need to work this out on your own." If these two people are your acrimoniously divorced parents, firmly declare that you won't pick sides. "You know I love both of you, so please don't drag me into your conflict; it's not fair to me." If they ignore your request and keep bugging you, suggest that they go to couples counseling if they need a third party so badly.

You might also see this in reverse; children often learn to triangulate their parents against each other to get what they want. "But Dad lets me smoke weed in the backyard with my friends all night when I stay at *his* house," a triangulating teenager might say to his divorced mother.

The key to dealing with Control Freaks is firm boundaries. We will explore boundaries more fully in part 3, but for now, think about where you draw your own line and what your limits are. Once you are clear on what they are, state them with noncombative firmness. Delineating where you stand might be a challenge for you if you are used to caving and complying with Control Freaks or more dominant personalities, which is what part 3 will help you with. First, here's a response to the example mentioned earlier:

TEENAGER: But Dad lets me smoke weed in the backyard with my friends all night when I stay at his house!

MOM: The rules you have with your father are not necessarily the same rules as the ones I'm enforcing in this house. When you're here with me, you need to respect my rules.

And here's a way to handle the possessive boyfriend mentioned earlier in the chapter:

BOYFRIEND: You're hanging out with Susan again? I don't like you spending time with that feminist nutcase.

YOU: You don't have to like Susan. I'm only asking that you accept that I like spending time with her.

BOYFRIEND: But she's a nutjob! I can't stand listening to her.

YOU: Then it's a good thing you aren't coming. I'll tell my nutjob friend you said hi.

That is your cue to exit. You don't need him to understand why you like Susan, and he doesn't need to be happy about your decision to go to lunch with Susan.

Of course, this is very different if you are in a domestic violence situation. If your partner is physically abusive and you fear that you are in imminent danger, consult with a therapist or counselor to create a safety plan, or contact a domestic violence hotline to ensure your safety.

You might feel as though you have no voice in your relationship with a Control Freak, but you are less powerless than you realize. The Control Freak wants you to feel stripped of power so that he can control everything and leave you feeling empty and out of control. While you cannot control how he will react when you advocate for yourself, you will always have your own set of choices. If he doesn't respect your boundaries, then you are presented with yet another choice: which might be to leave. You are the only one who remains in control of you—not him—despite what he might be leading you to believe.

Remember this:
The only realistic form of control is self-control.

Chapter 6

THE BULLY

A look behind the mask of intimidation: feeling diminished
Tactics used: control, intimidation, belittling, smear campaigns,
emotional blackmail, guilt and punishment, prize dangling

WHEN WE HEAR THE WORD BULLY, we usually think of a big, towering kid in the schoolyard picking on the smaller, timid kid sporting thick eyeglasses and a backpack that gets kicked open by the bully and his entourage of sycophantic meanies. We think of Biff from the classic film *Back to the Future*—the massive, hulking meathead who bullied Marty McFly's dad.

The truth is that bullies come in all sizes and all ages. They can be male or female, although they are more often male. A bully is defined as a person who habitually seeks to harm or intimidate those perceived as weaker or vulnerable in some way. Let's take Napoleon Bonaparte, the first French emperor and one of the most famous military generals in history, who happened to be fairly short (although, interestingly, not unusually short for the time period). The term Napoleon Complex comes from him and was inspired by his aggressive, fiery temper. It describes a person who compensates for their physically small stature by acting like a hothead. Bullies feel small and insignificant inside, regardless of their stature.

Still, though, not everyone who is or feels physically small becomes a bully, so why do people become bullies? Bullies often were themselves the victims of bullying. Many bullies were abused by an oppressive or cruel parent. Sometimes grown-up bullies were bullied as children outside the home and grow up to become adult bullies. Bullies fear weakness more than anything, and therefore they crave power. Feeling weak, small, and powerless deep down, they overcompensate with intimidation, overt control, and harsh criticism so they can reign over others instead of being squashed by others. Sadly, those are the only two options they can see. Perhaps high conflict and fighting for survival were the only coping mechanisms modeled for this person growing up.

Take Napoleon, for example. He was an Italian boy born in Corsica and sent off to a French boarding school in the late 1700s. He did not speak French fluently, and so the French kids teased and bullied him for his weird accent, small stature, and provincial, hillbilly behavior. Later, he became an unstoppable force and seized power over most of western Europe despite plots to assassinate him. Napoleon was viewed by his enemies as a warmonger, dictator, and usurper of power, and some accounts suggest that he was a psychopath. Without a doubt, Napoleon was a complex historical figure, but he illustrates the idea that bullies are essentially scared souls who have learned only to fight and to win; they see no other way.

The Bully trusts no one. His greatest fear is that others will try to control him and strip him of power. If you are in an intimate relationship with a Bully, he probably believes that nobody could truly love him or care about him because deep down he sees himself as inadequate or inferior in some way. He lives with a lurking emptiness that he doesn't know how to fill so he makes sure others around him feel weaker, lesser, smaller, and most of all, powerless. And also, stupid.

Since people are complex and all these profiles can blend together, maybe your Drama Queen or Control Freak with a raging temper feels like a Bully, too. The distinction between the Bully and all the others is that Bullies have a mean streak. They are sadistic and cruel. Your suffering gives them a boost. Most human beings like to wake up to a cappuccino or maybe add vitamin B to their smoothie to start their day; Bullies like to start their day with a good rumble. Kicking down their perceived opponent is invigorating for them.

Some Bullies are angry rageaholics; they have fiery tempers and anger problems. Often, people with anger problems were not given the space to process their emotions as children and therefore never learned how to properly grieve or express themselves. Anger is often fueled by other emotions that might feel too scary to express, such as sadness, shame, resentment, fear—all kinds of complicated emotions the person never learned how to process or tolerate. These emotions can make the person feel too vulnerable, so they shift into anger instead. People often resort to anger when what they are really experiencing is fear. Think about what a cat might do if trapped in a corner. That cat will usually hiss. The cat appears mad, but he's truly afraid.

These anger-prone, rageful individuals might not necessarily intend to bully others, but their poor impulse control causes them to snap and then, all of a sudden, their composure goes to hell in a handbasket. The tiniest ripple can set them off. They have enormous amounts of stored anger and resentment; they are one empty Twinkie box away from exploding. If you saw the movie *Zombieland*, then you might remember the scene at the beginning of the zombie apocalypse, as the world is coming to an end, when a hunky Hell's Angel–looking Woody Harrelson finally succeeds at busting open a Twinkie van, only to find a load of SnoBalls treats instead of Twinkies. This sends him over the edge because he doesn't like the stupid fucking SnoBalls, he just wants Twinkies, *dammmmmn it!*

People who succumb to road rage, for example, have short fuses and can instantly morph into bullies once they are provoked by strangers in their vehicles on the road. *Beef*, a popular Netflix series, is a great example. This fascinating show follows the aftermath of a road rage incident between two strangers that ignites an ongoing feud and brings out their darkest impulses. It realistically portrays how untreated depression and deeply harbored resentment can be inflicted outwardly and destructively.

Forms of Bullying

Getting bullied, in all its forms, can result in feelings of worthlessness, defeat, despair, and in some cases, depression.

- **Physical bullying** is the obvious kind. It includes a physical assault on someone's body or possessions, such as hitting, punching, kicking, tripping, shoving, and so on.

- **Verbal bullying** is the less obvious kind involving verbal threats and emotional blackmail. It includes mocking, teasing, name-calling, belittling, harassing, and various forms of scaring and shaming someone.

- **Social bullying** is perhaps the most manipulative form of bullying because it is insidious in its covert nature. This is also the one adult bullies most often resort to. It includes smear campaigns, humiliating the victim in public, spreading rumors, deliberately leaving the victim out in a social situation, or ostracizing them from the group in some way. Social bullying is the mean-girls phenomenon; there was even a cult classic movie about it called *Mean Girls* in 2004, followed by its remake in 2024, with a star-studded cast about a select group of shallow, elite high school girls.

- **Cyberbullying** is a growing problem that takes places via the internet. It involves posting harmful content such as nude photos, digitally retouched photos, and messages aimed at harming a victim. These days, smear campaigns are easier than ever to orchestrate using social media platforms. Never engage with a cyberbully; instead, block their account.

Like Water Off a Duck's Back

The best way to handle any type of Bully is to either completely ignore them or stand up to them. Never submit to them. Do not cower. Bullies are looking for targets, people who are easy to dominate. You need to show them they don't affect you at all. Remain unflappable. You are impervious. Simply glide along, minding your business as usual, letting the bully's terror fall off you like water off of a duck's back. In short, you don't give a fuck. Here's how to project *I don't give a fuck*:

- **Project confidence.** This is the number one key element, because projecting confidence is how you avoid bullies and predators alike in the first place. Your confidence is a huge deterrent; it tells them their plan to mess with you is going to be challenging, and all the Bully wants is an easy target. Be mindful of your posture. Don't walk around with your back slouched, head down, eyes on the floor. Stand tall. I don't care if you're four feet tall. Stand up straight and tall, chin up, chest out. Think Chesty Peacock; that is your new spirit animal.

- **Ignore them.** When a Bully starts bullying, ignoring them is one of the best strategies. Studies in behavioral modification show that one of the most effective ways to shape behavior is to ignore bad behavior and reward good behavior. By ignoring them, you aren't giving them any ammunition to keep going. You're giving them nothing to use against you. Also, it's no fun to play with someone who isn't playing along. Make it less fun and maybe they'll stop. This means you don't engage, and you don't react. You can change the subject if you want. You can walk away, you can get off the phone, you can turn around and talk to someone else in the crowd. Most importantly, don't take any of the shit they say personally.

- **Nip it in the bud.** We are going to talk a lot about boundary setting in part 3 of this book, but for now, what you need to know is that you need to set boundaries right away, before things worsen and spiral out of control. Confront a Bully immediately without anger or emotion. In this book I will frequently highlight noncombative firmness because that is the tone you should take when you are setting boundaries. You remain calm but firm, never hostile or aggressive. Logic is your friend. You might respond with a firm, "What did you say to me?" or "What do you mean by that?" Even better, you can ask, "Are you being rude on purpose?" This question lets them know you aren't afraid to tell them they are being rude, but it also gives them an opportunity to walk it back once confronted. It can be especially helpful to plainly describe their behavior in the moment like this: "You know what my name is yet you keep calling me 'fucktard,' which is extremely rude." Now, here comes the boundary: "I need you to address me by name or I won't respond." Boom.

- **Kill them with kindness.** The idea behind steady kindness is to demonstrate that you remain unstirred. If you were smiling and enjoying your day before your encounter with them, then make sure your rude encounter with them has little to no impact on your mood and disposition during and after your encounter. Imagine an invisible shield protecting you from their animosity. Try to feel sorry for them rather than let them upset you. You might say, "Are you okay?" and feign a concerned expression. Remember that this is an insecure person trying to feel powerful, if that helps you to take pity on them. Keep your composure while protecting your energy space. You might even look at them and say something like, "You must be having a bad day" or "I hope you feel better soon" and then ride off on your bicycle. This deflects the situation and also confuses the Bully.

The Office Asshole

Workplace bullies are common. They tend to prey on the most insecure, anxious, and cooperative workers. Bullies also target those with skills and strengths because they don't like to be eclipsed by someone else, which elicits feelings of inferiority. So they do things like try to steal your thunder, take credit for your work, undermine your work, berate you, belittle you, or dismiss you. Bullies who are skilled manipulators also use more subtle manipulation tactics. Examples of the more subtle tactics include the following:

- Finding ways to change your responsibilities to disrupt your work and undermine your sense of purpose

- Constantly shifting the goal post or creating unrealistic expectations to ensure failure

- Deliberately excluding you from meetings or work events or, oops, forgetting to invite you

- Hiding or distorting information to look better than you, ruin your reputation, or charge ahead of you to unfairly meet their end goals

- Pitting people against each other to create a divisive atmosphere (triangulation)
- Spreading office gossip (smear campaigns)

My client Hannah could be called a perfectionist. We spend a lot of time talking about her harsh "superego" (a Freudian term for being overly disciplined and hard on oneself) and how to talk to herself more gently. But I've also listened to her recount times when her unrelenting desire to perform has bitten her in the ass. In one case, she was targeted by an office bully who was intimidated by her polished skill set. Hannah accepted a new job in a more male-dominated department of a company where she had been working for a few years already. Nervous about joining a team of mostly men who might think less of her, she signed up for tons of online courses relating to her job. Hannah devoured as much educational and training material as possible. Soon after, she began turning in reports that outshone everyone else's, as you might imagine.

When the boss announced at the next meeting that he wanted everyone to write their reports more like Hannah's, you could almost see the proverbial spitballs and paper airplanes flying at the back of Hannah's head. They all came from one seething individual: the boss's grandson, who had been thriving in his nepotistic nest as the star of the department. From that day forward, he made sure to make her look bad at every meeting. When another boss whom everyone liked got fired one day for doing something stupid, this bully spread a crazy rumor that Hannah had accused him of sexual harassment, which is what had gotten him fired. You know, to make sure that nobody would like her, and any guy who didn't want trouble would probably avoid her too. And also, who knows, maybe she would quit. But she didn't quit. She approached him confidently. Without accusing him of anything, she asked him how they could improve their work relationship and added that she wouldn't tolerate rude remarks, lies, and rumors. He was speechless and then mumbled that he didn't know what she was talking about (gaslighting). Instead of debating what had or had not happened, Hannah insisted that professionalism was important to her and that she would do whatever was necessary to clear up any confusion with him or anyone else to ensure a harmonious work environment. She thanked him for listening. And glided along. The conversation was awkward for sure, but happily for Hannah, the bullying stopped after that little chat with the Bully.

Hannah showed the office bully that not only had he failed to intimidate her, but that he also didn't have the power to ruffle her feathers. Remember, think Chesty Peacock. Channel your new spirit animal before a confrontation, if that is what you must do. Also, get creative with whatever works for you. If you're not feeling the Chesty Peacock, go with something else. In Hannah's case, she remembered a middle school teacher named Mrs. Meyers, whom she looked up to and admired. Mrs. Meyers was always able to get the class to settle down, even the worst of the little delinquents. She spoke in a firm, even tone and commanded respect in the classroom. Hannah imagined that the bully was one of those unruly little boys and she was this teacher. She spoke with firmness, feeling her grip on the situation the same way Mrs. Meyers had a grip on that classroom. The idea is to visualize and channel whatever works for you.

Bullies are looking for easy targets. Standing with confidence and setting firm boundaries at the onset of any disrespect will minimize your risk of getting bullied. If you struggle with those ideas, don't fret, we will get there ahead.

Remember this:

Let self-confidence be your superpower. And don't let anyone take it from you.

And this:

A real boss (Eleanor Roosevelt) once said, "Nobody can make you feel inferior without your consent."

Chapter 7

THE PATHOLOGICAL LIAR AND THE CON ARTIST

A look behind the mask of make-believe: an unbearable truth

Tactics used: gaslighting, projection, stonewalling, playing the victim,
word salad, prize dangling

IF YOU ARE IN A RELATIONSHIP THAT has you playing "detective," you are
most likely dealing with a pathological liar or a master manipulator
of some kind. You know you are playing detective when you find
yourself constantly checking his friends and followers on social media
and snooping through his phone or devices any chance you get—or
you desperately want to do those things. If an artist were to draw you
in cartoon form, you'd be portrayed peering through a microscope
with one sharp eye while puffing your pipe under a deerstalker hat.
Obviously, this is not a normal way to behave in a relationship, and
yet this is how you find yourself behaving if you are dealing with
someone who is incapable of telling the truth. Your reaction is your
gut telling you something is deeply wrong. Your partner's actions just
don't add up. Their words don't align with their actions. They lead you
down an endless trail of excuses with an infinite stream of other people
to blame. Their stories are convoluted and baffling. If you question

them, you are labeled paranoid, jealous, suspicious, controlling, and annoying. You are told that you are harassing them when you ask them about their empty promises.

People lie for many different reasons. Different personality disorders and types of mental illness are associated with lying, although lying itself is not a disorder. Each disorder has distinct and specific motivations for lying.

- Narcissistic Personality Disorder (NPD)—When someone has NPD, their lies tend to involve either grandiosity or exploitation. Essentially, they are lying to look good, restore their image, preserve their false identity, hide a blunder, get out of trouble, prove they are right, get something from you, get you to do something they want, or present themselves as the conquering hero or the pitiful victim.

- Borderline Personality Disorder—When someone with borderline personality disorder lies, their lies and manipulation are usually frantic attempts to avoid rejection or abandonment. They do not necessarily intend to consciously manipulate or deceive people, but their manipulation is often an impulse to get their overwhelming needs met the only way they know how.

- Antisocial Personality Disorder—This disorder is usually associated with criminals and con artists. Their motivations, like the narcissist's, tend to be exploitive. Their lies involve fraudulent activity, using aliases, pretending to be someone else entirely, and deceiving others for personal gain. They are less concerned than narcissists with their image and more concerned with their end goal.

- Factitious Disorder—This unique disorder is specifically about pretending to be sick. It has a variation of Munchausen syndrome by proxy that is specifically about pretending someone in their care is sick—for example, a mother falsely pretending that her child is perpetually sick. They fake symptoms of illness that result in years or even a lifetime of medical appointments and hospital stays for no personal gain.

- Active Substance Abuse—When someone has untreated drug or alcohol addiction, honesty will often fly out the window because this person's primary motivation is to get high. Using the substance on which they are chemically dependent can feel to them like a primal need, so all other priorities and obligations recede in importance. They are usually convinced that nobody could possibly understand how badly they need to keep using their drug, so they resort to lying to obtain, keep using, or hide their drugs. Unrecovered addiction can completely transform someone's personality, lifestyle, and relationships. The good news is that honesty and accountability become real possibilities when the addict is committed to their recovery.

- In a broader sense, other cases of pathological lying may have developed as a coping mechanism resulting from family trauma. Such cases happen when people grow up in dysfunctional or abusive homes and experience neglect or severe criticism. If mistakes or flaws are deemed unacceptable, and individuals learn to believe they are not good enough, then they may begin to believe lying is their only way to get their needs met.

Let's examine the types of liars you might encounter. These types may or may not involve mental illness. Here, we focus on their motivation for lying so you can use appropriate strategies to deal with the specific type of liar you encounter.

Brands of Pathological Liars

THE AVOIDANT LIAR

The Avoidant Liar is arguably the most benign of the bunch. This person is afraid of confrontation and copes with that by telling you what they think you want to hear. They are not malicious or intentionally deceptive. On the contrary, they are people pleasers who cannot bear disappointing others. Many people do this in some form.

The Avoidant Liar is your perpetual yes-man, promising to have brunch with you after he already promised breakfast and lunch with other people on different sides of town. Later on, he has to let at least one person down that morning when he realizes he can't be everywhere at once. He really wants to be everywhere at once, though. The Avoidant Liar is your friend who tells you that the bleached mullet you're sprouting because you don't have time to go to the hair salon looks good on you, or that the canary-yellow skinny jeans are so "you." Those may be fairly harmless little white lies, but at times they can also be frustrating.

The more hurtful lies are the omission lies, when they decide not to tell you stuff that they should be telling you; this includes things that might make you mad. They don't tell you that they talked to their ex-girlfriend for an hour last night or that they gave their phone number to a cute guy in line at the grocery store. Why risk it?

Many of us can identify with this fear of confrontation, especially when we are around dominant personalities. You, as the reader, might identify with feeling anxious and find yourself hiding, omitting, or sugarcoating the truth around your partner. I'm not trying to pick on you. I'm illustrating a dynamic. Bear with me for a second.

Avoidant Liars are fearful and anxious. And if you understand that, then the next question should be this: What are they afraid of? In this context, we know it's confrontation. But why? What are they afraid might happen in a confrontation? Here is where it gets interesting and variable because the answer could have something to do with how you react to them, or perhaps how other people have reacted to them in their past. They might withhold delicate information because they have been conditioned to do so by you, their previous partners, their parents, or a combination thereof. If you want this person to be honest with you, you need to create a safe space for them to express things that might be upsetting to you. This will give them a chance to be more honest with you.

Practice slowing down your reactions. Ask questions that remove all traces of accusation and blame. Show that you are grateful for their honesty. Applaud their courage for sharing something that might upset you. Validate their feelings if they conflict with yours. Let them know it's okay to have these feelings, even if you don't like what you are hearing. Express a willingness to compromise or come to a resolution, instead of doing the things they fear the most—yelling at them, shaming them, or rejecting them for sharing their honest feelings.

For example, don't say, "You gambled a whole week's salary away in Vegas again last week?! See? You can't be trusted with money, you loser!" Instead, slow down. Ask them what happened. You can calmly tell them you are disappointed that this happened again, without berating them. Share your concerns. Ask questions about what might help them be more financially responsible in the future. Otherwise, you can be sure the next time they lose money at the blackjack table, they will "forget" to mention it to you. Make it safe.

THE NARCISSISTIC LIAR

The Narcissistic Liar is more complex; they somehow justify their deception as an acceptable way to achieve their end goal, even at the cost of your feelings and ability to trust them. They lie for many reasons.

False Image—They lie to maintain their shining image as the conquering hero so you'll continue to admire them. They might also be playing the sad victim to arouse your sympathy and pity, as a way to get their needs met. Either way, they craft stories for self-aggrandizing purposes. Poking holes in their stories usually inflames the situation, triggering anger and defensiveness.

Magical Thinking—Narcissists thrive off of feeling special and amazing, which means they can become delusional in order to protect their fragile egos. In such cases, they resort to magical thinking. People often want to know whether narcissists *actually believe their own lies*. Yes and no. Yes, they know full well that they are lying, but also, they desperately need to believe their story; in a way, they are lying to convince themselves as well as you. They tend to repeat their stories over and over again as a way to ingrain them in reality. Over time, the stories solidify and feel increasingly real to them each time they repeat them. After a while, the line between fact and fiction begins to blur heavily. They can also find clever ways to justify their deliberate deception: "You see, I had to forge my mom's signature on some of her checks because she's too senile to pay half of her bills . . . Oh, the check that was made out to me? I don't know what you're talking about."

Power, Control, Domination—The drive to reign over others at all times presents the liar with a need to distort facts to maintain their superiority and all-knowing status. Lying helps them win arguments. Lying is a shortcut to achieving instant credibility and status. They make empty promises to keep you on the hook or to appease you in the moment, but they rarely follow through. The few partially materialized promises, usually very small ones, are nothing but a tactic to keep you under their control by sustaining your trust. This prize-dangling manipulation tactic is used most commonly by narcissists and con artists. Keith Raniere, the sex cult leader described in chapter 5, used the prize-dangling tactic when he promised his followers special promotions within the levels of the twisted operation he was running. He dangled the golden carrot at all times to get his people to jump through crazy hoops to attain the splendor they were promised. The

intermittent reward of advancement for some of the members contributed largely to the continued energy investment of the members.

Escape Accountability—Narcissists don't own up to mistakes,
and they will lie their pants off to cover their tracks. They tell lies
to escape scrutiny or criticism of any kind. They hide even the most
mundane mistakes as carefully as fugitives burying bags of money in
the ground. Lies are weapons to protect their flawless image. They
throw up smokescreens of deception and speak to you in a word salad
so incomprehensible that you'll throw your hands up in defeat. The
really smart ones can sound like they swallowed an encyclopedia when
they spout technical "facts" to confuse you.

DEFENSE TACTICS

When dealing with Narcissistic Liars who often gaslight you, deny
or distort reality, and swear by their own fiction, it is important to
understand that you can't make them tell the truth. Their bullshit is
a defense mechanism designed for their survival, so there is no successful way to tamper with that. Try your best not to participate in
their bullshit by trying to convince them that they are wrong. Liars
don't admit to lying. If they are capable of lying about what happened,
then they are capable of lying about lying. If you can't ignore them
entirely, remain neutral and stay calm. If you do decide to challenge
their lies, keep your composure and maintain noncombative firmness.
The objective is not to try to force them to tell the truth; you cannot
change how they are wired. Instead, your objective is to stay grounded
in *your* truth and let them know they can't sway or manipulate you.
Phrases like this will keep the conversation from escalating:

- Your recollection of events differs greatly from mine.

- It is clear that we just don't see things the same way.

- Thanks for sharing your perspective of what happened.

- While I can't control how you feel about me, I do feel that your perception is misguided.

- You have a right to your own point of view, as do I.

- What you're saying simply doesn't match what I observed firsthand.

- I hear what you're saying, but that is not what is written here / what I can see in this photo (present evidence).

- It's okay if we don't see things the same way.

- This conversation doesn't feel productive.

- I would rather talk about this more calmly. Let's hit pause and revisit this another time.

- Good talk. I really have to go now.

Anytime the conversation escalates or starts to feel hostile or spiral out of control, disengage and shut it down, as suggested in the last few bullet points. Narcissistic Liars are ready to gaslight anyone who scrutinizes or criticizes them. They often project you or your reliable witnesses as liars. They can become belligerent, defensive, or dismissive. Don't let this get you upset or worked up; instead, use this as your cue to shut it down and protect your energy space. Mentally note their unhealthy response and let that be useful data to inform your continued trust and investment in them.

The Con Artist

The Con Artist is a sociopathic imposter without a conscience. How does a human being become a Con Artist? Author Maria Konnikova describes the grifter as a composition of the dark triad of traits: psychopathy, narcissism, and Machiavellianism. The Con Artist may have one or all of these traits, or any combination thereof. Let's break this down.

Psychopaths are biologically predisposed to exploitation and have an absolute indifference to suffering. Clinical studies show that they lack a physiological response to shocking or disturbing experiences that would have most humans' pulse racing or body temperature rising—like serial killers who callously and nonchalantly chop up human bodies in their leisure time. Don't worry, psychopaths account for an estimated 1 percent of the population.

Narcissism presents the ego-inflated elements of grandiosity, entitlement, self-enhancement, and manipulation; narcissists do whatever it takes to preserve their image and get what they want. This egocentric trait of self-promotion at any cost is a factor driving the behavior of the Con Artist.

Machiavellianism, considered the most relevant trait for the Con Artist, is a personality trait centered on the ruthless manipulation and exploitation of others; they are naturally talented liars with no moral compass, zero empathy, and no remorse. They are callous and calculating. Unlike narcissists, however, they are not interested in attention, admiration, or self-image; instead, they are all about winning (or stealing) the treasure.

Con Artists conduct schemes ranging from multimillion-dollar Ponzi schemes to small-scale frauds that rob regular people of their livelihoods. You've probably heard of "Anna Delvey," who made headlines for posing as a fake German heiress among the New York elite and was sentenced to prison on eight charges involving fraud and theft. If you watch the television series based on her story, note how many times she repeats "the money is coming" to all the people subscribing to her nonsense.

How do Con Artists get away with their schemes? First, they locate easy, vulnerable, unsuspecting targets. Con Artists are extremely perceptive; their discerning eye can read the vulnerability all over a person's face and body. They are enterprising mind readers who morph themselves into whatever they perceive their targets need in the moment. The make-believe Prince Charming is perhaps the most commonly encountered con artist.

Dirty John, a scammer, drug addict, criminal, serial con artist, and suspected sociopath whose true story was captured on Bravo's thriller series, shows how a master manipulator can cunningly work his way into a vulnerable, unsuspecting woman's life, causing a nightmare that tore apart her family. A wealthy interior designer and four-time divorcée with a hunger for real connection, Debra thought she had found the real deal when she met a handsome "doctor" who swooned over her. The relationship took off at warp speed. Despite the sharp concerns of her two adult daughters and other family members from whom he attempted to isolate her, she married him swiftly and secretly, which granted him access to her abundant finances. Gradually, her fairy-tale romance unraveled into a reign of terror, especially after she discovered that her dreamy doctor was actually a nurse anesthesiologist who had lost his license after stealing drugs from hospitals. Eventually, her charmer revealed himself to be a pathological liar with a nasty temper and a criminal past involving a jail sentence and a long history of abusing, stalking, and conning women. This nightmare ends with a disgruntled John attempting to kidnap Debra's twenty-five-year-old daughter at knife point as a culmination to his threats, acts of violence, and violations of restraining orders. Luckily, the young woman fought back hard, wrestled for the knife, and stabbed him multiple times; he died from his wounds.

Many stories like this one involve a con artist who manages to lure an innocent, trusting person into his grip and then succeeds in alienating them from their family or anyone close to them. The Con Artist starts by vilifying the family members to each other, driving a wedge between each family member, and essentially triangulating them. The manipulator consistently repeats messages over and over until they solidify into nuggets of truth. He gives his target messages such as, "Your children don't appreciate you." Or he tells others living in the home: "Maybe it's time for you to move out." This is how Con Artists get their chosen victim all to themselves where their victims are increasingly susceptible to their word, which makes it easier to manipulate them.

You can observe this phenomenon of message-planting triangulation in a harrowing docuseries called *The Puppet Master: Hunting the Ultimate Conman*. This is the true story of a brazen con man named Robert Hendy-Freegard who masqueraded as a British spy in Europe. He manipulated people and stole large sums of money from his target's families, leaving behind a trail of destroyed lives. You may find it shocking to watch people become totally brainwashed and turn against their loved ones while under the spell of a madman, but it happens all the time.

TRICKS OF THE TRADE: SIGNS YOU ARE GETTING CONNED

- **The Reciprocity Trick**—When a relationship is new, the con artist will appear to be full of generosity. What they are really saying is, *I'm doing all this stuff for you, so I expect your loyalty in return.* If you feel like you owe this person, and they are asking you to do something you are not comfortable with, don't get tricked into performing out of obligation. It's a subtle form of emotional blackmail. It's wonderful to reciprocate if you have a genuine desire to do so, but don't do it out of obligation.

- **The Peer Pressure Trick**—I'm not just talking about meanies in middle school. The need for social validation exists at any age or stage of life. If you are feeling pressured to behave a certain way, appear a certain way, or do something inauthentic to yourself in order to fit in, gain someone's approval, or keep them from leaving, you are getting manipulated. That's a good time to pause and rethink the situation.

- **The Now or Never Trick**—Act fast! *Call the number on your screen now, and we will throw in a free wooden spoon while supplies last!* We've all heard a commercial like that or seen the warning when shopping online that the product in our shopping cart is going fast; check out now before they run out! Creating pressure with no time to think is one of the oldest tricks in the book. Anytime someone insists that you must decide in a split second with no time to reflect because that offer will no longer be available, it is often a scam. Reasonable people give you time to think. Con Artists don't want you to think about anything long enough to realize you are getting conned.

- **The Postponement Trick**—"The money is *commmmminnnng!*" But in the meantime, you're expected to shell out a large sum, pay for an extravagant din-din, or hold the vacation on *your* credit card just until their "bank issues" get resolved, all with the promise, implicit or explicit, that you'll be rewarded for your trust and loyalty. When someone has a thousand excuses for the delay in what has been promised to you, it might be time to consider that the promise is empty and the prize does not exist.

As you can see, people lie for a myriad of reasons. Pay attention to when someone's stories don't add up, sound outrageous, or contradict what you observe. Also, don't ignore your intuition. I'll be talking more about this later.

Remember this:
A lie repeated over and over doesn't make it true.

Chapter 8

THE WOMANIZER

A look behind the mask of charm: an intimacy-phobic predator
Tactics used: breadcrumbing, belittling, control, projection,
gaslighting, ghosting, love bombing

THE WOMANIZER. Otherwise known as an emotional predator, player, playboy, fuckboy, Casanova, serial monogamist, ladies' man, smooth operator, skirt chaser, heartbreaker, and more.

This chapter is for the ladies. Wait. As I say that, I realize plenty of women can be charming heartbreakers too. Some of them seduce you and use you and then throw you away when they are done. Women manipulate people just as men do. Some of them are just looking for affirmation and want attention from men who want sex. And there it is: sex. This chapter is about men who don't want any emotional attachment and will use the female desire for emotional attachment to get sex. And yes, of course, women might do that too. But in this category, men are the overwhelming majority, so we are focusing on the men womanizing women.

"How you doin'?" is the cheesy yet unforgettable pickup line uttered by the charming, girl-crazy Joey Tribbiani from the popular '90s sitcom *Friends*. A cute, dimwitted, struggling actor who lives for meatball sandwiches and girls, Joey is hard to be mad at. Not all Womanizers are bad guys, but all bad boys manage to break a girl's heart.

Many women have been stuck in a confusing relationship with a man who is considered emotionally unavailable, commitment-phobic, afraid of intimacy, or married. The Womanizer goes through dates like Tic Tacs; the purpose of each date is simply to score in the sack. Sometimes they are honest enough to let women know right away that they are not interested in a relationship and just want casual fun (fair enough), but others will keep women on the hook with the right lines and irresistible charm.

The Rationale behind Womanizing

The reasons for this phenomenon vary. Sometimes it's simply about an ego boost. Getting the girl shows the Womanizer that he's important. Men who need this ego boost badly enough to bed women for sport are most likely Egomaniacs. They are seeking constant praise and affirmation that they are amazing. The dating arena is just one of the many ponds where they fish for compliments.

For others, it could be the disease of more. Men with addictive personalities might selfishly want instant gratification all the time. Sex and Love Addiction, a disorder characterized by an impaired ability to engage in healthy intimacy, might be the reason why a Womanizer is pursuing multiple women at once or why something feels off. The addict's preoccupation with sex and fantasies forms a barrier between the addict and another person. In other cases, they might not necessarily be sex addicts or love addicts or sex and love addicts, specifically, but if they are an addict in some form, they might just get carried away with the thrill of instant gratification during certain life stages. This usually happens when they are young and the game of chase feels easy. Addicts will often succumb to the disease of more, even if the object is not their vice. Think of the alcoholic in recovery with a desk drawer full of candy bars because he can't have just one of anything.

Some men womanize and cheat because they are obsessed with controlling women. (Flip back to chapter 5 for a refresher on Control Freaks.) With regard to womanizing, the art of seduction is a game that keeps the Womanizer in control of women, so none of *them* are ever in control of him. In some cases, these men are experiencing unconscious anger and hostility toward women. They might appear to love women, but they love them the way a fox loves chicken. Women are prey. For a real misogynist, women are the enemy they must conquer. It's about holding the power position above all else. Real intimacy requires reciprocity and equality—words that would make a misogynist gag.

If you examine the family history of your Womanizer, you can usually learn why he operates this way. The way his parents behaved with each other as well as how they treated him will influence how he sees women. For example, let's take Mom. If she was overbearing and controlling, he might grow up with the fear of being suffocated. The example of love, closeness, and intimacy he was presented with felt stifling. The last thing he wants is to be in love with a woman because he imagines she will suffocate him. He has learned that if he doesn't obey, he gets punished; therefore, he would rather avoid responsibility and obligation to someone else. He would prefer to be a free agent, with nobody to report to. Now let's take Dad. If the Womanizer's dad cheated on his mom, abandoned the family, lived a double life, or ran off with his young, hot secretary, womanizing behavior was modeled for him. He learned that manhood means escaping a woman's control.

There are countless ways this might have played out in the Womanizer's past, but the point is that by avoiding intimacy and keeping you at bay, he is in control instead of under your control. But maybe none of these reasons are the real reason why your Womanizer womanizes. Maybe he is just selfish. Sometimes that's all it is.

Here are some of the ways Womanizers do their womanizing:

- **Breadcrumbing**—When they are stringing you along, and most likely a few other women, they can't give you all of themselves, so they spread themselves around by leaving you just a few crumbs. This might look like the occasional text that says very little and never asks you out. This is the "what you doing?" text at midnight, or the "hey stranger" text after you've just about given up. If you are not getting consistent or frequent contact, chances are he is not "all in" and he's breadcrumbing you. These are also the guys who call you once or twice a month to hook up. You are most likely on rotation with a couple of other girls with whom he is doing the same thing. If you are dating to find a real relationship, don't put up with this. Let them know you need more continuity to stay invested in seeing this through, and be ready to end it if they are not capable of that.

- **Ghosting**—When they completely disappear without warning, you have been ghosted. The Womanizer halts all forms of communication, hoping you will get the hint so he doesn't have to act like a mature grown-up and talk about it. This is a lot like stonewalling or the stone-cold "silent treatment," which is ridiculous, weenie behavior. As an advocate for direct, clear communication, I prefer to handle this by straight-up asking them whether they are ghosting you. "Hey, wondering what's up with you, been a long time. Are you ghosting me?" You can add the ghost emoji, LOL, or something to make it light and playful, which creates more safety for them to reengage. If they didn't mean to ghost you but just felt embarrassed about how long they took to reply, you're inviting them back in and letting them know it's safe. Of course, your ghoster might still stay silent, but in that case, now you know what the deal is. That should help you move on.

- **Haunting**—After they ghost you, it can be confusing when they still watch or react to your posts on social media. They haven't replied to your text, but they just hearted the video of your cat Carlton eating corn on the cob with both paws. Okaaayyy? This can feel like a total mindfuck. Why are they doing this? They probably don't want to commit or get serious, but perhaps they sense that you do, so they avoid making plans but don't want to actually cut you off or burn that bridge. I would treat this the same way as ghosting. Ask them directly what's up if it feels important to you to know for sure. Otherwise, let it go and assume you are ghosted.

- **Stashing**—Another way to avoid a real commitment or keep you on rotation while retaining the other women in his life is to stash you, which means hide you and keep you separate from the rest of his life. If you're hanging out with a guy regularly and you're intimate and it feels like you're together, but you haven't met any of his friends, family, or coworkers, that's a red flag. Combine that with no pictures of you together on social media and no plans to meet anyone in his circle anytime soon when you have been seeing each other for a while, and you are probably getting stashed. You can safely assume you are probably not the only girl his dog, Captain, gets kicked off the bed for. If you feel like this is happening to you after several months of dating, start asking more questions about his personal life and pay attention to how he reacts. Does he share willingly or shut down the conversation? Talk to him about wanting to get to know his world and see what happens.

The Love-Bomb Effect

If your Womanizer seems to fit the narcissistic traits we have been talking about in this book, you might want to consider whether you are stuck in the cycle of abuse with a narcissist. Narcissists are known for reeling their targets in with what is referred to as the love-bomb effect. This is essentially the honeymoon stage, which is a phase of every normal relationship, except this one is the honeymoon stage on steroids pumped up with idealization, flattery, and constant attention. During this time, they manufacture a bond with you that breaks down your guard and alters your brain chemistry in such a way that you become addicted to the rapidly firing pleasure centers in your brain. You are hooked. The Love Bomber is essentially grooming you to become dependent on them. This is the initial stage in the cycle of abuse.

After you are riding high, convinced that they are riding high right along with you, they have you right where they want you. The higher you soar, the lower and harder you will fall. They pretend to share your values, hopes, and dreams. How amazing is it that you found another person who wants to build a petting zoo on a yacht in the Pacific Ocean?

You feel truly adored and cherished. They tell you that you are special and you are the one. But when they tell you that their ex was crazy, pay close attention. Was she crazy, or did he end up driving her crazy by making her feel this special only to devalue her and discard her with an earth-shattering thud?

The devaluation stage creeps in gradually and insidiously. It is not immediately detectable because devaluation incidents are gently peppered into the love-bomb stage. Love Bombers are often subtle and clever about their earliest devaluation. They continue to groom you with suggestions disguised as compliments, such as, "You're not insecure like my ex-girlfriend. She was so possessive and always had to know where I was." This is your warning not to ask him what he's up to. This is not praise; this is an expectation disguised as praise. This is control.

Once you appear to be effectively under their grip, the devaluation will pick up speed. Harsh criticism plants self-doubt seeds that grow over time with more and more criticism. Cruel jokes are thrown at you, but you are expected not to be "too sensitive." Your deepest insecurities are brought up only to be used against you. Arguments quickly turn explosive.

You are no longer a slice of perfection. What happened? It is not a mystery. Quite possibly, you have discovered *their* imperfections, which is intolerable to the narcissist. So they project flaws onto you to shield themselves from the necessary introspection that intimate relationships require. *Let's look at you, not me.* Basically, when they feel their own flaws seeping out, it's time to blame and devalue you.

This cycle typically continues on repeat until the ultimate discard. The discard occurs when the narcissist is done playing with you. Usually, they decide they are done with you once they feel too exposed. Your unacknowledged needs become an affront to their manufactured, flawless self-image. You caught them being imperfect. The jig is up, time to say goodbye. Off you go.

What's a Girl to Do?

I don't know where you are in this process, so let's talk about my client Sara, who was confused by her hot and cold boyfriend. He used to buy her romantic gifts, send her poetry verses every morning, and eagerly plan vacations together. Today, he's sitting at home smoking a doobie, texting her sporadically, and getting annoyed when she asks him why he has stopped making plans to see her. Once things got serious, he backed away. She wants to know what she should do now.

She has choices, but none of them involve making him do anything. Her choices are really about her, not him:

- She needs to decide whether she can accept the watered-down version of the relationship that he's giving her and create reciprocity by putting in less energy herself. This gives him the opportunity to recalibrate the relationship if he really does value her but was feeling overwhelmed by her expectations. If he does not recalibrate the relationship after Sara has explained her expectations and backed away, then she has her answer. He is not meeting her needs, and he probably isn't ever going to.

- She needs to evaluate what kind of relationship she wants to have. Let him know that the change in behavior doesn't feel good and doesn't work for her. Decide to end the relationship if this is all he is offering and if this is what she can expect moving forward.

Do not hang around in a relationship if you are being treated poorly, ever. Being alone for however long you have to be alone is how you value yourself and give yourself a chance to find what is truly right for you.

The longer you stay in a situation that does not serve you, the longer you postpone finding the situation that does.

Confessions of Two Womanizers

I got to talk to two self-proclaimed "pigs" about what they were like when they were in their heyday. They are gentlemen today.

TOMMY, FIFTY-TWO YEARS OLD, MARRIED

Tell me what makes you think you were a Womanizer?

Looking back, I always had sort of an addictive personality. As a kid, I didn't just go to the store to buy one piece of candy. I would buy all the candy the money in my pocket could get me on any given day. Once I realized that I could attract certain kinds of females, I took advantage of that, because I'm selfish and self-centered and wanted more of everything that feels good. It was a huge ego boost to be able to get girls. It made me feel like I was special, so there was a feeding of the ego. How many women I could get to like me boosted my ego and made me feel special.

Also, because I thought falling in love was so rare, why not just get as much intimate pleasure as I could, without committing or developing a relationship, I thought to myself. So, I would say whatever I had to say, and act however I had to act to entice someone to have sex. Looking back, it never felt right afterward. I just wanted to feel intimacy in moments, like tonight, not forever. Sometimes I would kiss them like I loved them. All because I wanted to feel that feeling.

Did it ever occur to you how she might interpret your make-believe feelings?

In the moment no, that is the self-centered part. It was pure, unmanageable pleasure seeking.

What do you think made you so selfish?

I think it's a—how can I describe it today—an extremely immature pleasure seeking above all else. Now I see this as emotional depravity.

For how long were you this immature?

Up to my forties.

Why isn't a man more mature in his forties? What keeps him from evolving into seeking a significant mature relationship?

The selfish part of my personality didn't go away for a long time.

What made you so selfish? What early childhood experiences shaped you?

Reflecting on the way I grew up, I think I was somewhat neglected, like an unattended garden. It made me feel like I had to just nurture myself. I wasn't taught the idea of nurturing and reciprocity. The only boy-girl info I caught from other people was from my peers—boys who were just as immature as me. There was no real guidance. My parents were great people, but they had zero impact on my relational skills. They didn't talk about things with me. I don't remember having one conversation about romance and feelings.

When did you feel things changing for you, and why did you stop womanizing?

When I actually fell in love with someone, I was about forty years old. It felt like real love.

What felt different this time?

I felt like she was unattainable in my mind.

How was she unattainable?

She was just as beautiful as the others, but maybe more independent. Things took time to evolve; her feelings were developing slowly. I knew she liked me, but I never felt like she was pushing the relationship forward. It allowed me to feel what I felt for her without pressure. The first time we kissed felt like an oasis, because I already knew I liked her before this moment happened.

So not feeling pressure from a woman you liked allowed you to warm up to the idea of a more serious relationship?

Yes. When you're not in love and a woman puts pressure on you, there is zero chance of it going anywhere—for me at least.

Do you hear that, ladies? Slow your horse down!

My takeaway: Many men, whether they are actual Control Freaks or not, have an adverse reaction to feeling controlled. Men with control issues, which is extremely common, fear losing their freedom and getting suffocated. Men like to pursue and conquer; it is wired into their DNA. They need to be the one to set the pace of the relationship. Feeling pressure from a woman feels like handing over control to her, which is a total turnoff for many men. The bottom line here is this: let the man work to earn your love and affection.

KRIS, FORTY-ONE YEARS OLD, SINGLE

What were you like when you were dating as a younger man?

I was into Brazilian jiu-jitsu, being fit, working out, and not giving a shit about relationships. I didn't really feel like anyone tripped my trigger, like none of the girls really did it for me, so I was just dating to date.

What do you think the girls you were dating thought was going on?

I think they thought it was gonna get more serious. We got to having sex pretty quickly, and once that happened, I knew I had the power. I didn't have to chase them anymore.

What did you do or tell them to make them think it would be serious?

I don't know, nothing. We would go out and have fun, and then I'd sleep with them.

Why do you think they slept with you so easily or so soon?

I was a good-looking guy. I was ripped. Sometimes I would offer to make dinner for them, so they'd already be at my place, and then we'd have sex. Or we would go out just for drinks and they'd invite me back to their place.

Did it ever occur to you at the time that you were leading them on?

Yeah, I was just interested in sex. I figured they knew what they were getting into so it wasn't all on me. I wasn't forcing anything.

Really—did they know? Do you think they realized there were no strings attached?

I didn't do it intentionally. I guess I didn't really think about what was going on for them.

When did that change for you? When did you start thinking about them?

There were a few times girls got really upset after I broke up with them. They would say, why did you sleep with me then? One girl, Ella, I will never forget. She told me while crying, "I never let a guy come inside me before you." And I was shocked. That was when I realized maybe they weren't just screwing around like I was. I realized I really hurt Ella. Later I regretted that.

What did you regret exactly?

That I didn't value her more at the time.

Why now, why do you want a serious relationship now?

I'm more open to letting people in than I used to be. When I think about who might have been good for me, I realize that I rejected good ones, like Ella. Also, I started wanting to have a family and kids before it's too late.

What made you decide okay, now is the time for that? Why not earlier, or later?

I saw that my friends had that. I looked at my life and saw I was drinking too much and wasn't taking my life seriously. I realized that I was fucking around and had to get my shit together, and so that's when I started to think about women in a different way.

Why do you think guys are Womanizers?

They get hurt once and then they are like, fuck it.

Did that happen to you as a young guy?

Yes.

Tell me.

I started dating an older woman. I was twenty-two years old; she was thirty-three. I fell in love, and I wanted to marry her—*why her?*—it was great sex, she was independent, confident, like she didn't really need any guy, so that made me want her more. But then she dicked me around. After we broke up, I got ripped, started competing in BJJ [Brazilian jiu-jitsu], and focused on my own goals and let girls chase me.

What advice would you give girls now?

Be straight up without being clingy. Don't play games.

They might say, but what if the guys play games?

Then don't play. If you're thinking they are playing games, then tell them how it makes you feel. I think if a girl did that to me, it might make me like her more because it would make me think wait, this girl might be cool.

Why? Because she is confident enough to speak up?

Yeah.

My takeaway: Confidence is everything, which is why we devoted a whole chapter to it. Here you have a guy whose confidence was shattered when the girl he wanted to marry rejected him, so he used girls for an ego boost while he worked on his biceps. But the interesting part is, he also admits that it takes someone with confidence, who values herself more than some guy and who speaks up about what's happening, to make him pause and think of her differently.

Remember this:

Never accept crumbs when you want the whole pie.

PART THREE

Becoming Bulletproof

Chapter 9

KNOW YOURSELF: HOW DID YOU GET HERE?

GAIL, A NURSE IN HER TWENTIES, came to my office with the idea of "trying therapy" because her friends were continually telling her that her husband is a narcissist and that his behavior is abusive. She wanted a professional opinion. I asked her to tell me about their relationship, what it was like at home. Without hesitation, she launched into a horrifying story about a guy who sits in the apartment all day waiting for her to come home from work, cook meals for him, and then clean up after him.

I asked her if he works from home, and she reported that he is unemployed and not even looking for a job. What does this loser do all day? He plays video games, watches TV, takes naps, and devours the contents of the refrigerator.

"Sometimes he wants takeout," she continues. "But when something is wrong with his order, he yells at me and insists that I go back and get him the right burrito. By the time I get home, I have to eat mine cold."

"What if you just refused to do that? What if you suggested he go back to get his own burrito? And deal with his burrito problem on his own like a grown-up?"

"Oh, he would just keep yelling. And it gets so loud and relentless that the easiest thing to do is go fix it just to make it stop."

When I asked her if he gets violent, she said flatly, "He doesn't hit me or anything like that." I kept eye contact with her and waited. "I mean, he throws things. Not at me, though." I kept waiting quietly. "Okay, he shoved me out of the way once when I was blocking the hallway." I quietly nodded without breaking eye contact, waiting for more. "He sometimes does this thing where he walks in the room and, like, whacks the back of my head when I'm working at the computer and calls me stupid. Not hard or anything. It doesn't hurt. But it startles me, and I find it annoying."

Annoying? It's *annoying* that he sneaks up on you and hits your head? There are better words to describe getting your head smacked on the daily for no good reason. *Annoying* would fit a scenario like he sneaks up on you and farts louder than a German jazz band. That would be annoying.

"When you use the word 'annoying,' it sounds like you don't find it totally unacceptable. It's like something you wish he would stop doing, but it's just one of those annoying things he does like fart or make dumb dad jokes."

"Oh, no, I've asked him to stop before, and he just laughs at me. Then he does it even more, and it only gets worse." She looked down as a wave of defeat washed over her.

Over the next few sessions, as Gail began to understand that her husband's behavior was indeed abusive, we worked on coping skills and assertiveness training. But we also examined how she had ended up with Biff Tannen for a husband.

"When can you remember feeling this helpless and trapped before? Was it like that at home growing up?" Gail divulged that she grew up terrified of her father, who had a raging temper. He used to repeat over and over that he regretted having her, and he would lock her in her room for hours. He criticized everything about her, calling her stupid, fat, ugly, and a huge disappointment.

Her mother was softer and kinder but was also the recipient of her father's abuse. She didn't know how to stand up for herself, so she wasn't capable of protecting Gail. Instead, Gail witnessed her mother do the same thing she did—tiptoe around an enraged tyrant.

Gail learned to play a placating role in order to stay safe. In her house, there was nothing she could do to make her enraged father stop going ballistic. Her only choice was to shut down, withdraw, placate, and do whatever it took to prevent him from erupting. She devoted herself to schoolwork and brought home nearly perfect report cards, hoping to prove to her father once and for all that she was not stupid. She hoped that doing everything he expected of her would ease the tension, although that never worked. Gail became used to being the recipient of someone else's anger. When everything is projected on you all the time and the only way to survive is by circumventing the anger of an emotionally unhinged human being whom you rely on for support, that's all you know. Gail learned that her survival was based on doing everything to please and soothe others and never, ever creating conflict.

While Gail's husband's behavior was disturbing, to say the least, it was familiar to Gail. Her caretakers failed to present a healthier alternative, so she didn't know anything different. Often, people are attracted to what is familiar, and that familiarity could be unconscious—we are drawn to it whether we like it and want it in our lives or not. This is why it's important to examine how our past has shaped us so we don't keep repeating the same pattern. It's one thing to be clear about what we want and don't want, which is a great start. But if we aren't also clear about what and where we come from and how that has impacted us, what coping mechanisms we rely on, and what role we keep playing with what type of person, then there is a tremendous risk of stepping in the same shit over and over again.

The Seduction of Familiarity

Many people, when pushed to reflect on a problematic relationship, can identify something about the relationship dynamic that feels familiar, whether at a conscious or unconscious level. If they think about it hard enough, it might mimic an interaction they experienced growing up at home.

Families operate like any other system with moving parts. Everyone in the system steps into a role to keep that system flowing. The role we choose, consciously or unconsciously, is shaped by our position within the system and what we learn from everyone else in the system.

We are given a unique personality the day we jump out into the world in our birthday suits. As we develop, we rely on our parents, caregivers, and even our siblings to help us navigate our interactions with the world. The guidance our family provided might be healthy or completely bananas, but whatever it looked like, it is the one we were given and the one that impacts us the most. The combination of the personality we are born with and the family environment shapes how we function and respond to the world, which could go a myriad of ways. Over time, we learn our place in our family system and take on a unique role that helps us thrive or survive in our particular environment.

Like most people, you likely stepped into a role that kept you relatively safe or got you the most attention, based on whatever everyone else in your family was up to at the same time. Most people figure out pretty early on what they need to do to stay safe, get rewarded, or stay out of trouble. As the family system continues to function according to everyone's established role, people tend to remain stuck

in their roles, which is what maintains the ongoing family dysfunction. And then, not surprisingly, they bring this same role into their
adult environment with others and attempt to develop relationships
in which they reenact their own family dysfunction all over again.

Unfinished Business: The Case of Maria

Maria, a middle child, felt rejected and ignored by her dad, who preferred spending time with her two brothers. Her oldest brother, who
had the most in common with their dad, went to business school and
went into the same line of work as him. The finance world provided
infinite ways for father and son to bond. Her younger brother became
the star athlete her father admired; he was the high school quarterback
and prom king. Weekends in their house were spent with half a dozen
men roaring at the sports channel with submarine sandwiches lining
the kitchen counter. Making money and watching sports was all her
dad seemed to care about. Unfortunately, Maria, interested in neither
of those things, never captured the interest or attention of her father.

Not coincidentally, Maria's last two relationships were with authority figures who seemed to single her out as special above the rest. In
college, she moved in with her philosophy professor at the end of
her senior year. When that relationship ended, she started dating her
boss at her first job after graduate school. In both instances, she felt
seen by someone important, and that filled her with feelings of her
own importance. She felt seen, validated, worthy . . . finally chosen.
The golden child, at last.

Freud called this phenomenon *repetition compulsion*. The wound
your family history left you with creates a search to heal it in a similar
relational pattern. Women who fall in love with emotionally unavailable men, or married men, might have had fathers who were absent,
neglectful, or abandoned them. They are driven by an unconscious

hope that maybe *this* unavailable man *this* time will be the one who finally makes them feel special and heals their childhood wounds.

Passed-Down Triggers

Consider how your family system, and your place in it, has shaped your emotional triggers. Self-awareness means not only understanding who you are and what you need, but also how you react and why.

Maybe you notice that you panic or feel disproportionately hurt when someone isn't there for you. If your parents were emotionally unavailable, you might be navigating your adult world with an anxious attachment style, meaning you feel anxious when someone fails to show up for you. Maybe you notice that you are quick to anger when it seems as though others are not listening to you, which might be related to feeling unseen, ignored, or dismissed in your childhood, perhaps stuck in the shadow of a louder sibling. On the contrary, if you find yourself pushing people away and getting annoyed when anyone tells you what to do, you might have felt smothered by an overbearing parent who invaded your personal space. Since this can play out a myriad of ways, reflect on your trigger buttons and how they get pushed. I don't know what your unique triggers are, but the idea here is to make sure you know what your triggers are before a manipulator has the chance to monkey with them.

What Draws Us to Narcissistic People?

We understand now that narcissists go to great lengths to avoid any reality that evokes shame or contradicts their fantasies of grandiosity, superiority, and power. But they can't do this in a vacuum. Narcissists need people to play along; they need people to praise them, appease them, serve them, and pump their ego a thousand different ways.

Many of us are willing to play along, perhaps without knowing exactly what kind of web we are getting pulled into, because there is something we need, too. Just as narcissists are trying to regulate or avoid their suppressed shame, sometimes we are trying to fill a void with their excitement and grandiosity. We are lured into their narcissistic trap by our own desire to feel alive and worthwhile. This can be especially true if you find yourself pulled into a love-bombing phase of seduction with a narcissist. See chapter 8 on Womanizers for more about love bombing.

Nobody enters a relationship with a narcissist looking to get abused. Most people have no idea that their seductive partner is narcissistic to begin with. Narcissists and manipulators turn on the charm, and they know exactly what to say and do to draw you closer. Too many times I've heard baffled victims say things like, "But he was so nice to me in the beginning" or "She didn't seem crazy at first." No shit, why else would you go back for more?

Being chosen by someone so charming, grandiose, and seemingly important in some way can feel reaffirming, even exciting. The narcissist offers something very enticing to others at first. While this is especially true if something feels missing in your life already and if your self-esteem is not intact, absolutely anyone can fall into the trap of manipulators and narcissists.

Now You Can See What Potentially Draws a Narcissist to You

Think about what role you play in social situations. How far back can you remember playing that role with people? Consider how your family position might have shaped how you relate to others.

Family roles can change over time or blend together. The list of roles we play in our family is endless: the identified patient, golden child, parentified child, lost child, scapegoat, black sheep, peacemaker, clown, mascot, hero, enabler, caretaker, troublemaker . . .

The role you played in your family is a result of your unique personality in combination with your social environment and a variety of other factors. Birth order, parenting styles, environmental factors, and many other factors impact how you decide to navigate your social environment.

I narrowed an inexhaustive list of family roles into three broader categories of personality traits. Most people will find themselves to be a blend of two or maybe even all of them to some extent. Read through the roles to see whether one of these archetypes resonates the most for you or which of the three fits you best.

More categories exist than just these three, and narcissist or egomaniac is not captured here. This list was designed to help you see, without judgment, how you might have been shaped through your family system, without shaking a finger at anyone. The three traits I see develop most often within families are people pleaser, perfectionist, and wallflower.

THE PEOPLE PLEASER

People pleasers are the peacemaker, caretaker, enabler, clown, mascot—basically any role that diffuses conflict. These people can be very skilled at deflecting with humor or else they learn the art of diplomacy, assuaging egos and fiery tempers with the right, perfectly chosen words.

If you identify as a people pleaser, you must have learned how to stay safe or get rewarded in your family by keeping all parties happy. Maybe someone in your family was a pain in the ass and everyone orbited around them; maybe your mom or dad or a sibling demanded a lot of attention. You were most likely the second, middle, or youngest child who had to squeeze yourself into an already established group. You likely watched your older sibling fight with one or both of your parents and decided to try things a different way. You benefited from your later arrival, which gave you the opportunity to observe how the system was already operating and decide on your place in it. If you didn't have any siblings, maybe your mom or your dad was difficult to get along with and you learned how to appease this parent by being agreeable and making sure to never disappoint them.

People pleasers learned early in life to put their needs aside and, instead, figure out what others need and accommodate them. If you are a people pleaser, you get so used to doing this that you tend to forget you even have needs of your own. When you are caught in the middle between two squabbling loved ones and you're asked, "Well, what do *you* want?" you find yourself shrugging and thinking, *Gosh, I don't know.* You don't know because it's something you have stopped considering. You are probably a charming, likable, and easygoing person. Quite possibly, you are doing all the giving in your significant relationship and getting frustrated with how imbalanced it feels.

THE PERFECTIONIST

Often the golden child, the parentified child, or the hero. You must have figured out that your ability to perform and achieve is how you got rewarded or what kept you safe in your household. Or maybe you had to be the responsible one because nobody else was, not even your mom or dad. Most commonly, though, perfectionists endured a parent who was sharply critical and demanding, even if it was combined with love. Today, your identity is probably tied to your work or another source of feelings of achievement.

If you identify with the perfectionist, you felt constantly pushed to achieve when you were growing up. It felt like no matter how well you were doing, one or both parents still imagined how you could be performing better. This instilled a need to always get things right and never screw up. We all know there is no such thing as perfection, and yet you still find yourself aiming to be the best, with internal narratives like *mistakes are intolerable* and *giving up is shameful*. I wonder if this mentality is what makes you afraid to give up on a toxic relationship. Perhaps leaving them would signal that you made a mistake choosing this person and were unable to make it work, so instead you throw yourself into fixing something that cannot be fixed.

THE WALLFLOWER

You are the lost child or the scapegoat. You were trying to slip by under the radar because getting noticed meant getting in trouble. Over time, you got used to blending in with the furniture to stay safe. Today, you are uncomfortable being the center of attention and would rather stay in your shell.

When the people you trust or turn to for protection are the same ones who terrify or reject you, you learn to shut down and ignore what you feel. If you identify with the wallflower, you might have learned that it is not safe to express your feelings. The fear of disappointing or offending others seems to come at a huge cost. The high-stakes situation at home can result in people pleasing, withdrawing, or a combination of both in adulthood. Your introverted, shy personality might be simply genetic, but if your childhood environment was volatile and anxiety provoking, then there is the added component of learned avoidance. Withdrawing and avoiding is what kept you safe, so that's what you continue to do in most places you go. Unfortunately, retreating and running from conflict is most likely not serving you in your adult relationships.

Caretakers and Co-dependency: The "Too Nice" Diagnosis

All the personality types previously discussed, especially and most obviously the people pleaser, aim to please in some way and therefore risk succumbing to co-dependent patterns. This is what I like to call the "too nice" diagnosis. We all want to be "nice," but your kindness is not for everyone all the time. Kindness without limits is unrealistic, and that should not be your goal. Instead, we should aim to please others while also taking care of ourselves and maintaining the appropriate balance. We should pay close attention to boundaries—not just your own, but also the boundaries of others. Narcissists and master manipulators don't like boundaries, so when they find people who are not good at maintaining them, they have hit the jackpot!

Narcissists and master manipulators love co-dependent people. It's easy to imagine why. Think of all the satisfaction one can get out of a person whose main goal is to please. The aspiration to be perfect, polite, and pleasant and to never let anyone down becomes exhausting and anxiety-provoking, and yet caretakers can't help themselves. Caretakers want to rescue everyone. Everyone but themselves, that is.

The word *caretaker* sounds a lot cooler and friendlier than it actually is. Caretakers are not just taking care of other people; they are also neglecting themselves at the cost of taking care of other people. Furthermore, sometimes taking care of other people means trying to control other people, often because those people are not willing to change or help themselves. This leads to co-dependency.

Whitney Cummings, a stand-up comedian and actor from Los Angeles, will tell you about the "endless quagmires" her co-dependent impulses have landed her in. Her most entertaining account is, undoubtedly, about the Australian stripper she met once. The stripper inspired Cummings into an immediate rescue mission to find the scantily clad dancer a job in TV production and a pathway to

U.S. citizenship. One sob story about an abusive boyfriend followed by a half-naked twerk and Whitney just couldn't help herself. The Aussie stripper must not have needed Whitney's rescue operation that badly, however, because after everything Whitney put in place to help this girl, she never followed up by email. Whitney, herself, in her own hilarious memoir called *I'm Fine . . . and Other Lies*, will tell you that she learned on her personal journey that this experience really captured the frustration about co-dependence: "We think we're helping, but the truth is most people don't need, don't want, or feel patronized by our 'help.'"[1] Stripper stories aside, she admits to having stayed in unsatisfying relationships for years too long, just to avoid hurting someone else's feelings.

Most people think of alcoholism and addiction when they hear the word co-dependency, and they are not wrong. Loved ones of addicts often become co-dependent as they try to manage their loved one's illness, monitor their consumption, and control their behavior—not because they are manipulative control freaks, but because they are anxious about what will happen if they don't. They get pulled into the pattern of fixing, changing, or rescuing this person, to their own self-detriment. Addiction is not the only co-dependent– fueled relationship, because addiction is not the only toxic behavior. When you find yourself preoccupied with changing, fixing, helping, or rescuing another person for any reason, you might be in a co-dependent relationship.

Co-dependent people have a knee-jerk reaction to helping other people, to the point of taking responsibility for other people's behavior and their problems. They often anticipate the needs of others and rush in without being asked. They do things for people they don't even want to do but feel a pull and can't help themselves. They do things for people who are perfectly capable of doing those things on their own.

---

1   Whitney Cummings, *I'm Fine . . . and Other Lies* (New York: Putnam, 2017), 32.

They try to fix people's feelings, speak for them, suffer consequences for them, and solve problems for them. They make excuses for them. They cover up for them. They give way more than they receive.

In the dating world, you know a co-dependent by the way they fall off the grid the minute they are in a relationship. They lose themselves and morph into whatever their partner is or expects from them. Your vegan friend who hates watching sports is suddenly cheering at football stadiums with Brad, eating hot dogs and pepperoni pizza. Your "indoorsy" friend who refuses to brunch with the flies outside on the patio is now sleeping with the mosquitoes in the dirt under a tent on a camping trip with Josh.

Let's get one thing straight: co-dependent doesn't mean that two birdies in love are enjoying a ton of quality time together. Time can be factored into the equation, but co-dependency has more to do with your level of emotional involvement and lack of boundaries. It is defined by a frantic need for approval, an inability to tolerate disappointing others, a preoccupation with the comfort of others, and your own overwhelming guilt and anxiety when you're failing to please everyone at once.

Are You a Co-dependent?

Co-dependents are characterized as caretakers with low self-esteem who tend to repress their feelings while focusing instead on rescuing other people. They struggle with issues regarding obsession, repression, control, dependency, poor communication, weak boundaries, anger, and more. The following is a long but inexhaustive list of clues that will help you assess whether you struggle with co-dependency. This list covers a variety of areas, so you might find yourself identifying with some of it, parts of it, or nearly all of it. See how many of these co-dependent tendencies you recognize in yourself.

How many of these are true for you?

When other people have a problem, I experience the following:

- I feel guilt, anxiety, or an overwhelming amount of pity.

- I feel compelled to help them solve their problem.

- I often do everything I can to fix or solve their problem for them.

- I immediately offer suggestions or solutions.

- I give advice, even if they did not ask for it.

- I try to fix their feelings or work hard at cheering them up.

- I get annoyed or upset when they don't take my advice.

- I feel responsible for making them feel better or helping them in some way.

- I feel sorry for them in a way I can't shake and forget about.

- I often wonder why other people don't help them the way I do.

- I feel the need to drop everything to respond to their problem or crisis.

- I skip my own scheduled activities or rearrange my schedule to help them.

- I feel resentful about how much I do for them.

In general, I find myself doing the following:

- Anticipating the needs of others

- Saying yes when I mean no

- Doing things I don't really want to do but feel a call of duty or obligation to do

- Doing things for others that they are capable of
  doing themselves
- Overcommitting, double-booking, or overextending myself
- Feeling pressure around certain people
- Feeling attracted to needy people (or they are attracted to me)
- Feeling driven crazy by other people and their bullshit
- Feeling used, underappreciated, or victimized by other people
- Worrying about ridiculous little things
- Losing sleep over other people and their problems
- Checking on people excessively

I often experience these feelings:

- Indecisiveness
- Helplessness
- Like I'm not enough
- Different from the rest of the world
- Ashamed of who I am
- Unlovable or discardable
- Undeserving of good things
- Guilty about spending money on myself
- Guilty in general or about a lot of things
- Like I can't do anything right
- Like a victim in a lot of ways
- As though others are never there for me the way I am for them
- Regrets about the past

- Threatened by the loss of certain people
- Trapped in relationships

I tend to do the following:

- Stay too long in relationships that don't work
- Blame myself for things that go wrong
- Control events, situations, and people out of fear of what might happen otherwise
- Feel controlled by other people
- Let others decide where we're going, what we're eating, what we're watching, etc.
- Ignore problems or deny that there is a problem
- Pretend things aren't as bad as they are
- Make excuses for people
- Lie to myself
- Believe other people's lies
- Automatically think I've done something wrong or upset someone
- Worry that others are upset or offended by me
- Experience situations that feel totally out of control
- Snoop or check on people to catch them doing what they're not supposed to be doing
- Engage in compulsive behaviors myself (binging, overspending, pill popping, drinking, etc.)
- Notice my stomach tightening into a knot much of the time or when interacting with certain people

- Look for happiness in other people
- Latch on to other people as a source of comfort, satisfaction, and overall happiness
- Center my life around other people
- Seek love from people who are emotionally unavailable
- Expect relationships to bring me the happiness I'm seeking
- Relationship hop, going from one shit show to the next
- Put up with bad behavior because I don't want to be alone or face rejection
- Get myself in real messes and sticky situations
- Ignore whether someone is good for me or healthy to be around
- Worry that people will leave me, stop loving me, or get terminally sick of my shit
- Fixate on saying the right thing the right way
- Ruminate and chew on things endlessly
- Take a long time to realize how I actually feel about a situation
- Have sex when I don't want to
- Engage in sex acts I take zero pleasure in and would rather not be doing
- Prefer giving rather than receiving
- Cover up, even lie to protect a person or problem
- Wonder why my problems don't go away or why there is always a problem

Reflection

If you identified with much of what you read in the list, or if you are still questioning your co-dependent patterns regarding a particular person or relationship, ask yourself these two questions:

- Do you want this person to change more than they do?
- Are you trying to help them more than they are helping themselves?

These two questions should help you reflect on where you draw the line between supporting someone and rescuing someone. If your answer is closer to yes than no, you might want to examine your co-dependent patterns.

Journal Opportunity

To help yourself explore this even further, see what you come up with when reflecting on these awesome questions:

- What would you be doing with your life if you weren't focusing on getting this person to change?
- How would your life be different if you were not in this relationship?

Remember this:

Wherever you go, there you are.

Chapter 10

SHARP COMEBACKS: HOW TO SET CLEAR BOUNDARIES

CASSIE'S PHONE IS RINGING IN HER PURSE AGAIN, and she's staring at it like it's a ticking time bomb that she doesn't know how to dismantle. "I already know it's my mother calling," she says with a panic-stricken face. When I ask her why she's afraid to answer her mother's call, she tells me that her mother has been blowing up her phone all day. "She wants to talk about my dad again. They're going through a divorce. They had a fight about selling their vacation home in Florida. It's a long, boring story, but my mom wants me to call my dad and talk him into keeping it for some reason. I don't want to be involved."

"Then don't get involved," I answer. Cassie says it's not that easy. Her mom is persuasive and forceful, like a jackhammer. "Have you told your mom you don't want to be involved?" I ask. Cassie shrugs. "Why don't we try that now?" After we rehearse and role-play her boundaries, she calls her mom back.

"Hi, Mom . . . Yes, I heard your messages. About that. Look, I don't want to be involved in your dispute with Dad . . . Of course I am part of this family, I'm your daughter, but I have no part in your conflict with Dad about your finances. You two are going to have to work this out without me . . . One more time, Mom, I am asking you not to embroil me in your conflict with Dad. It makes me very uncomfortable . . . Okay, well, if you can't accept that, I simply won't stay on the phone when you bring this up because it puts me in an unfair position. I hope you understand . . . Okay. I'm sorry you feel that way, Mom. I love you very much, I have to go now, bye." Boom. That's how it's done.

First, let's talk about what boundaries are not. Boundaries are not about controlling or changing anyone else's behavior. Your boundaries are not ultimatums or demands, which insist that other people change instead of you. If your boundaries sound like a demand or some kind of threat, people will bristle at feeling controlled, and it usually won't go well for you. And your happiness and well-being should not depend on someone else's behavior anyway.

Your boundaries have nothing to do with other people's behavior. They have everything to do with you and how you take care of yourself. When you set a boundary, you are letting other people know what you need—all the while understanding that they are not obligated to meet your needs. Healthy boundaries include understanding that when you make other people aware of your needs, you give them a choice—to either meet your needs or not. And their decision to meet your needs or not also gives you a choice. You get to choose what you will allow or tolerate. You get to decide whether you want to stick around or hightail it out of there. Everyone has their own set of choices.

If the concept of setting boundaries feels uptight and annoying to you, try to think of it this way: Boundaries are opportunities to keep people in your life. Your boundaries define who you are, how you see yourself, what you value, what you believe, how you treat others, and how you let them treat you. Setting your boundaries allows them to learn about you, how you function, and what it takes to have a good relationship with you. This is how you collaboratively work to maintain your relationship. If others are ignoring or disrespecting your boundaries, it allows you to see that the relationship cannot thrive, based on what you are learning about each other.

Here's another helpful way to look at it. Boundaries define where you end and where others begin. Each one of us is a separate entity, but people with weak boundaries often struggle with maintaining that separateness. Some people invade boundaries, and some people don't protect their own boundaries very well. That's where relationships can get into trouble. The person who fails to set boundaries ends up feeling resentment toward the person enjoying the rewards of their lack of boundaries. Harbored resentment is not only a relationship killer, but it leads to feelings of anxiety, depression, and worthlessness. If anything, set boundaries with people so you don't end up resenting them.

The following table has some examples of what healthy boundaries sound like, next to their rude counterpart:

Ultimatum/Threat/Demand	Healthy Boundary
If you loved me, you'd stop smoking weed.	I am not comfortable being in a relationship with someone who engages in daily drug use.
You need to be nicer to my friends.	It's important for me to be with someone who can get along with my friends and family.
If we don't get married next year, I'm breaking up with you.	I'm interested in the kind of commitment that is headed toward marriage, so I need to know if we are on the same page.
If you won't clean up after yourself, you should move out!	I try to keep a clean environment. I can't see myself being happy sharing a space with you long term if we can't get a handle on the shared clean-up chores around here.
You need to go to therapy!	We have tried to work through our issues on our own without much progress. Would you consider seeing a therapist, with or without me present?

Your boundaries will have more impact if you state them calmly and firmly. You need to maintain self-control for a boundary to work; if you don't, it's all too easy for the other person to flip things around and point to you as the crazy one. Remember, manipulators use projection and gaslighting tactics like they are scratching an itch in their sleep. Don't give them the ammunition to use against you.

If you are yelling, sobbing, or delivering your boundary with excessive emotion, people tend to focus more on your tone, delivery, and mood than on what you are actually saying. I know this is easier said than done; our emotions so often get the best of us. If you are screaming at your partner, for example, your words might be brilliant, but there's a pretty good chance he won't hear them while he's busy thinking, *Why is she screaming at me? When will she shut up already? Is this ever going to end? I hope the neighbors can't hear us.*

So, keep your cool for maximum impact. Here are some tips and guidelines to help you maximize your impact while setting boundaries.

Boundary-Setting Tips and Tools

THE CHESTY PEACOCK

Conceptualize, if you can, the discussion about your boundaries as an opportunity to practice your own self-control and poise. You absolutely need to approach this discussion with calm, unwavering confidence. You might remember the Chesty Peacock from chapter 6 on Bullies. When you want to stand tall with confidence, think of a Chesty Peacock. They're standing there, chest puffed out like, *Yeah, I got this, don't nobody mess with me. Besides, I'm too pretty to fight with you.* Since you need to approach these confrontations with confidence, think about embodying a Chesty Peacock. If you're not a fan of that image, pick something else. Stepping into the persona of someone you admire for their calm confidence can be quite helpful. It doesn't matter who that person is. It can be your spirit animal, a heavyweight champion boxer, or your awesome grandma. Whoever it is, step into that energy.

THE SHIT SANDWICH—WITH A NICE, JUICY PICKLE

Nobody wants to eat a shit sandwich. But if you build a sandwich with some nice bread, maybe some fresh ciabatta, and throw in a juicy pickle, the person you want to confront might be able to take the, um, unpleasant part along with everything else. That said, it's always a good idea to lead with empathy. Build a positive framework before you deliver a message they might not want to hear. The first thing you say should be something they do want to hear. And it is especially effective if it reflects how they might actually be feeling or what they want you to know or understand about them. People are more likely to listen to someone who understands them. For example, "I know the first thing you want to do when you get home is throw all your stuff down after a long day, and I get that . . ." (before your boundary about putting things away).

HOW TO AGREE BEFORE YOU DISAGREE

As part of building a positive framework to get your person interested in hearing what you have to say, highlighting something you already agree on can be helpful. You are starting off on the same page, and you come in looking less like an opponent and more like their team-mate. For example, "I agree we have to cut back on spending. We are spending way too much money, aren't we? (Now he's listening.) Here's my concern about your idea to cut back on the kids' summer programs. I see us spending our time this summer as the referees to three loud, little delinquents zooming through the house at all hours of the day while we are trying to work. I would rather put them in a camp, maybe a less expensive one, and see if we can make a budget cut somewhere else."

If you can't come up with a single point to agree on, you can make yourself sound more agreeable by at least agreeing on the importance of the topic. "I agree that we need to talk about this" or "I agree that this is important." Finding ways to use positive language like "I agree" or even "You're right about (this part)" creates the framework for a more collaborative dialogue.

LEAD WITH YOURSELF

It's not usually a good idea to start any kind of confrontation with "you." Starting with "you" sounds like the beginning of an attack. *You were late again. You never clean up around here. You were flirting like crazy with that girl. You raise your voice too much. You don't call me often enough.* Those are terrible ways to start a discussion. The first thing out of your mouth should not be a blameful attack or an accusation. If you begin a conversation by telling someone all about how they are fucking up, the dialogue is unlikely to go in the direction you want.

Opening with "I statements" instead can remove the blame and shame sound to your message. Instead of starting off talking about their behavior, start with yourself and describe how their behavior makes you feel: "I don't like to be kept waiting" or "I find it hard to listen to you when you raise your voice."

Personally, I like "we statements" even more than "I statements" whenever possible because it reinforces the idea that you are on the same team. When you issue attacks and blame, you immediately become opponents, which sets the stage for a juicy fight. Alternatively, when you say, "We should be more careful not to raise our voices when we talk to each other" or "We need to work at staying calm when we disagree," you are essentially removing the accusation that *he* raises his voice, and instead you are suggesting that it is important for both of you to work on it, which sounds more like teamwork than a brawl. And it's true. Whether *you* raise your voice or not, you both need to constantly work on it; he might need to even more than you do, but you can leave that part out. Nobody's in trouble now. Defenses don't need to go up. This creates a safer atmosphere for discussion.

ALWAYS AND NEVER

Lodging a complaint with the words *always* and *never* are surefire ways to trigger a defensive reaction. They come off sounding like an exaggeration, and the other person will likely bristle at hearing you place them in such an extreme category. Don't say things like, "You never think of anyone but yourself!" or "You're always on your phone." Instead, bring up the most recent instance, and talk about how you feel without attacking the other person. If you want to talk about the frequency at which the issue occurs, you can say this is something that happens often, or that it has happened before, and so it is worth bringing up. If you say *always*, all you're gonna get back is this: "That's not true! I don't ALWAYS do that!" Look what a dumb argument you've just landed yourself in; now you're stuck backtracking out of "always" into an accurate rate of frequency with an angry guy who is not even listening to you anymore. Don't fall into that trap.

Say you successfully keep *always* and *never* out of the conversation, yet the other person still gets defensive. Maybe they fire back with, "All you do is bring up the past!" as a way to escape accountability. Don't let that derail you; hold firmly to your point about the change you would like to see. Clarify that you are not concerned about the *past*; you are concerned about the *pattern*. You might say, "I am actually

less concerned about the past and more concerned about the future."
And then ask for what you need moving forward.

MATTER OF FACT

State your boundary by clearly communicating an observable fact that
conveys what you see as a problem, how you feel about it, and what
you need or want to move forward. The delivery must be devoid of
blame, judgment, and emotion. This formula is less likely to trigger
a defensive reaction. These statements begin like this:

When I *am kept waiting for a long time* . . .
When I *see crumbs on the kitchen counter* . . .
When I *hear shouting* . . .

All these statements are followed by your feelings, such as, "I feel
frustrated." Finally, you can end with a request, such as, "I would like
you to give me a heads-up when you're going to be late."

THANK YOU IN ADVANCE

A helpful idea that can create a positive experience for everyone is
to thank them for doing what you want them to do before they have
actually done it. Kind of like, at the beginning of a meeting, when
you thank attendees for taking the time to meet with you and share
their thoughts with you. You don't know how much time they will
really give you and whether they'll share any helpful information.
But saying so in advance makes them feel good about the possibility,
so maybe they will.

For example, my twenty-three-year-old client was about to quit
her miserable job in a toxic work environment. She didn't have another
job lined up, but she couldn't take it anymore. When she informed
her parents, they cautioned her against quitting before she had any

other offers. My client explained why it was important for her mental health to quit immediately. She explained that she did not have offers, but she had interviews lined up that she felt optimistic about. Then she finished by thanking them for their concern, and especially for always being so supportive. They stopped arguing with her about quitting too soon. Instead, they wished her luck in finding something quickly. When you plant the seed that you see the person in a positive light, as someone who is likely to support you, they naturally want to accept that compliment and continue to support you. So thank them for what you need. Thank them for listening. Thank them for caring about the issue, even if you disagree. Thank them for being open-minded. Thank them for understanding. Thank them for anything you can think of that feels real in that moment.

Boundary-Setting Tools in Action: Hijacking a Funeral

I attended a strange funeral once. When the father of my friend Doug passed away, he was the one who organized a memorial that took place mostly over Zoom because the family was spread around the globe. His sister, Dana, had cut off the entire family for almost twenty years and moved to Canada; she claimed that everyone abused her after she joined some kind of cult or participated in a hippie therapy ritual following their mother's death. Doug wasn't sure what had happened to Dana, but he was convinced nobody in his family was abusing anyone. If anything, Dana was the most dominant, difficult, and controlling family member whom his mother had spoiled and enabled, giving into all her demands just to avoid conflict.

You can imagine how surprised Doug was to find Dana appear in her little Zoom box at the memorial of their father, a man she vociferously loathed. It was the first time Doug had seen her in nearly two decades. Family and friends gave their introductions, and each shared a memory about Doug's father. When it was Dana's turn, she announced that she had created a family photo album that she wanted to share. Doug asked her to wait until everyone took their turn to speak. Once she was given the ability to share her screen and begin her presentation, all the guests were forced to turn their attention toward her photo album as she narrated what was going on in great detail, spending several minutes on each photo. She went through photo after photo. Eventually, it became clear that she had no photos of their father in the album, although she did manage to pepper her presentation with a few snide remarks about him. Highlighting all the times her father was absent, she told elaborate stories about literally everyone in the extended family, except the deceased man the memorial was meant to honor.

Flustered, Doug sat in the room surrounded by his wife and kids and a few supportive friends; they were all nudging him and each other to address the hijacked memorial. Doug didn't know what to say. He reluctantly tried to interrupt his sister several times, but she kept projecting loudly over him, turning the pages of her toxic family project and continuing her disrespect of their father. Doug remained motionless, terrorized by his disturbed sister.

Finally, after the sister had droned on with this nonsense for about twenty minutes with no end in sight, Doug's wife, Charlotte, walked over to the computer, hit the mute button, and stood before everyone to make an announcement. "I need to interrupt the photo album adventure, which is a wonderful collection of memories and deserves its own separate family event. Dana, thank you very much and feel free to send a group email to everyone if you would like to organize that. For the sake of time, I would like to bring this moment back to focus on the reason why we are all here, which is to commemorate the life of my father-in-law. We will now disable the screen share and take a few more minutes to remember him before we wrap this up."

See if you can identify any of the tips and tools from earlier that can be found in Charlotte's boundary at the end of this story. If you noticed the shit sandwich, you are correct.

"When Shit Happens" Series

The following is a collection of examples that illustrate creating boundaries in a variety of settings. These come from my clients, my friends, and just about anywhere. Maybe you can relate to some of these.

WHEN THEY INSIST ON TALKING ABOUT SOMETHING YOU ARE NOT COMFORTABLE WITH

When you have conversations with people, you are not on the witness stand before a judge and jury. You don't have to answer every question someone asks you. You get to choose which topics you would like to participate in and which ones you want no part of. It's perfectly okay to shut the conversation down. Maybe someone asks you something too personal on a first date, or maybe your hothead friend with strong political opinions asks you who you are voting for over lunch. You can shut it right down before it begins. There is no rule that says you have to play along. Give yourself permission to say any of the following statements:

- No comment.
- I would rather not go there.
- *I'm not going there* (to be even more emphatic).
- I would rather talk about something else.

- Now let's talk about something else (if they aren't listening).
- Change the subject on your own if they don't listen to your boundary.

These responses are about you, what you need, and what you want; they have nothing to do with them. It's perfectly okay to let them down with your lack of participation in their chosen topic. People who appreciate you and respect you actually *want* to hear what your boundaries are because the last thing they want to do is dictate where the conversation will go or invade your boundaries. If people don't like your boundaries and continue to push back with their own selfish agenda, they are most likely the people who have been taking advantage of your lack of boundaries in the first place and will continue to do so if you let them. Anyone who ignores your boundaries does not respect you, plain and simple.

WHEN THEY ARE YELLING AT YOU

People raise their voice for a lot of reasons, and many aren't even aware that they are raising their voice. They might have a short fuse, have ADHD, have anger problems, or been affected by trauma. Maybe they snort cocaine all day. Maybe they don't realize they are shouting.

Whatever the reason might be, you want to first assert yourself by setting a boundary and explicitly stating that you won't tolerate such a high volume. Make sure to focus on their voice or tone and not on them (remember not to start with the word "you"!), so they feel less attacked. You might say, "Do you mind lowering your voice? It's hard to focus when your volume is that high."

If they continue to scream right over you, say their name loudly to get their attention, and then restate your boundary. "Travis! Hey,

Travis! I'm having a hard time following you. Can we take the volume down a notch?" (See how I used "we" in there instead of "you" to soften the blow?)

If they still keep yelling, get ready to shut it down and disengage. "We need to stop and revisit this conversation when things have cooled down." After you let them know you won't continue, disengage immediately by leaving, hanging up, or exiting.

WHEN THEY ARE PUTTING WORDS IN YOUR MOUTH

People speaking for you and labeling your intentions can feel so frustrating. Stay calm when you hear maddening remarks like, "You're just doing this because . . ." or "You obviously don't care about me" (a Drama Queen's favorite line). Resist the urge to shout back defensively. A much more effective strategy is to calmly point out that you will speak for yourself, by saying statements like this:

- I'm happy to speak for myself.
- I'm the one who gets to decide how I feel.
- Those are your words, not mine.

If they continue to rant and rave, let them tire themselves out, and then interject this: let me know when you are ready to hear me speak for myself.

WHEN SETTING A BOUNDARY WITH A NARCISSIST WHO LITERALLY DOES NOT CARE ABOUT WHAT YOU NEED

Asking a narcissist to pay attention to your needs can feel like beating your head against the wall. They aren't the least bit interested in catering to your needs and desires because they are strictly and solely preoccupied with their own. But sometimes you might really need a narcissistic relative or coworker to do something or stop doing something. What you might try to do then is show them how your request aligns with *their* needs and desires, which tends to consistently be about looking and feeling great. See how you might be able to show them how doing this thing or stopping that thing will make them look good in front of others. Press their self-image button as you craft your request, and make it sound like your request is an opportunity to enhance their image. See if you can find a way to make them appear as the hero, the genius, or expert extraordinaire in this scenario, and it might work.

WHEN YOU ARE LISTENING TO A BULLSHIT, LAME-ASS APOLOGY

"I'm sorry you feel that way" is not a real apology because they are still escaping accountability for their actions. They put the focus on your feelings instead of their actions. Let them know you hear the difference by saying, "I hear that you are sorry for how I feel, but I still haven't heard you say that you are sorry for what you did."

Another variation of this kind of bullshit apology is the "I'm sorry if I did anything wrong" line because the "if" gets them off the hook. It suggests that their wrongdoing is up for debate; maybe they did something wrong, maybe they didn't, maybe it's all in your head. You can repeat back, "*If* you did anything wrong? You mean you still don't know what you did?" And then be ready to clarify your position calmly and firmly to them. Let them know that for you there is no if and that you're hoping this conversation will result in a better understanding of what you're expecting them to apologize for. And look, this person is either capable of understanding it or not. Lack of empathy and narcissistic traits will shield them from that level of reflection, so when you hit that wall and it's not going anywhere, just drop it. At that point, they are simply showing you their deficient capacity for empathy and mutual respect, and you need to accept their deficiency. In situations like this, the best option is usually for you to let go of receiving the apology you deserve from an individual who is incapable of that level of emotional maturity.

WHEN YOU ARE RECEIVING UNWANTED ATTENTION

Don't be afraid to burst some horny guy's bubble right away. If you don't drop the sledgehammer, he will persist, and his attempts will only pick up speed. Here's an example that my client Lila had been dealing with until we crafted a response to finally shut it down.

Lila, an attractive, twenty-something personal trainer, goes to the gym every day and talks to most of the members there. Most gym members know who Lila is, even if she hasn't landed them as a client, because she is so outgoing and friendly, greeting everyone with the same big smile. Each day, the same white-haired old man with a big belly is sitting in the corner, playing around with the kettlebells. One day, Lila greeted him with the same smile she gave everybody and said she saw him there every day. Before she could mention his exercise routine, he jumped in to ask her if she was single. She said no. He asked for her number anyway. She politely moved on. Over the next few days, this man started messaging her through her social media accounts, insisting that she go on a date with him. She ignored all the messages. He bombarded her relentlessly, exclaiming how strange he found it that she had approached him, said she noticed him, and now wouldn't even respond to him. *What is wrong with you?* he finally wrote.

Obviously, Lila needed to set a boundary immediately. Lila responded to his last message: "What is wrong, sir, is that I approached you in a professional environment as a professional, and you continue to ask me on a date, despite my clear lack of interest in this type of interaction. Please stop harassing me." That is the last and only message Lila should ever have to send to this man, and if it escalates any further, she can report him to management at the gym. Don't be afraid to become harsher when someone is harassing you.

Narcissists do not engage in healthy communication because they aren't interested in anyone else's perspective, particularly when it conflicts with theirs. They don't respect boundaries because they are only interested in their own feelings and their own experiences, not yours or anyone else's. These communication tools are for you. If they help you improve your communication with your partner and other people in your life, awesome! On the other hand, if you don't notice any progress with a person who continues to disrespect your boundaries, then it should be clearer to you than ever that you are dealing with a very toxic person who is not capable of change.

Remember this:

Put on your own oxygen mask first.

Chapter 11

INVISIBLE SHIELD: HOW TO DETACH

SCOTT WAS SOBER FOR FIVE YEARS, until his fortieth birthday, when he decided to drink again. But this time, he was going to drink like a gentleman instead of a Viking. He just wanted to be able to order wine on dinner dates or have a beer once in a while with his friends.

When he met Laura, he was stopped dead in his tracks, taken by her beauty and poise. He feared this gorgeous, younger woman in her early thirties was unattainable. He made sure to present the best version of himself and hid his dark alcoholic past from her. He ordered the finest wine on their first candlelit dinner date.

The chemistry between the two was electric. They fell madly in love. They eventually talked about sharing their futures together. But over the course of time, Scott's drinking began to accelerate. Laura was convinced that when they booked a trip to Mexico, he was going to pop the question. She had always fantasized about a romantic, surprise wedding proposal on an exotic beach. The trip, however, did not go as she had imagined. Scott would wake up each morning to spiked-coffee breakfasts. He would float in the pool with a can of beer all day, wash dinner down with insane amounts of tequila, and pass out. No sandy strolls on the beach at sunset, and certainly no surprise engagement ring.

The relationship deteriorated as Scott's drinking increased. He started to act like a completely different person: picking fights, becoming irrationally jealous of other guys, and suddenly backing out of his earlier desire to move in together, without any real explanation. Laura had no idea that the real reason he wanted to live alone was so he could drink unmonitored—his drinking had returned to its previous unmanageable state. She did notice that his drinking was excessive and that the more he drank, the more the relationship suffered. She mentioned this observation to Scott only to be met with sharp defensiveness and gaslighting remarks.

When asking Scott to reduce or stop his drinking didn't work, Laura was sadly left with no choice but to end the relationship. Laura had tried everything to repair their relationship and help him see his unhealthy choices, but nothing worked. Setting a firm boundary, she told him that she was uncomfortable with how much he was drinking. He had been acting like a completely different person for several months, and the relationship no longer felt healthy and good for her. She added that if he wouldn't stop drinking or get help, she couldn't be with him anymore. He continued to insist that he didn't have a problem and begged her not to leave him.

The hardest part for Laura was what followed after she broke up with him: practicing detachment while the man she still loved was texting and calling her, begging to see her. She told him she would not see him or speak to him until he had thirty days of sobriety. She continued to ignore his texts for months and months, until one day he texted her an image.

This story actually has a happy ending. (Some stories in life will, and some won't.) When Laura opened the image, it was a photo of him holding his thirty-day sobriety chip at an AA meeting, standing next to his proud sponsor. She agreed to have lunch with him after that. He has stayed sober and exceeded his previous five-year record, and they have since gotten married.

The point to this happy ending is that you can't control, fix, or rescue anyone. They have to decide to make a change for themselves. And when someone appears to be uninterested in changing, there is absolutely zero motivation for them to decide to change as long as you keep hanging around. Why would they? Your presence, no matter how upset you are, gives them implicit permission to keep doing what they are doing because you are still there. As long as they have one person to keep bullshitting, they will keep on bullshitting.

Here is the bottom line: detaching yourself from someone's harmful or toxic behavior allows you to protect yourself and find out what they are capable of without your unhealthy caretaking.

What Does Detachment Mean?

Detachment means letting go. More simply, and perhaps more harshly, it means minding your own business. Detaching doesn't have to mean you don't care. It means that you care but you don't lose your mind scrambling to fix everything for someone else. Detaching while caring is a balancing act. When you fully understand where you end and someone else begins, detachment becomes easier to practice. You learn to focus on your own feelings and responsibilities, and you let others do the same. You realize that whatever is happening inside the six inches between someone else's two ears is none of your concern.

Detachment involves no longer making someone else's problem your own. It means no longer making someone's crisis your own drop-everything emergency. It means you release the desire to rescue, fix, or control someone, and you stop acting on that desire.

If you find yourself going into panic mode about how mean or how selfish they might think you are for setting boundaries, remind yourself that you have no control over how they will perceive you. Some people will choose to remain unhappy with you and your choices no matter what you do, so trying to make them happy becomes pointless. If you know you are making good choices that respect yourself without disrespecting other people, it's perfectly okay if someone else does not like your choices.

But It Still Looks Like I Don't Care . . .

Let's make an important distinction here. You can care *about* others without caring *for* them. While it is appropriate to care for your young children who cannot care for themselves, it is not always appropriate to care *for* capable adults. When we appropriately care about adults instead of caring for them, it means we care that they feel a certain way, but we are not doing for them what they are capable of doing for themselves. Caring about others does not always require that we give up what we need or want just to keep the peace. We care about how sad they will feel when we break up with them, but we don't stay in the relationship longer and make believe everything is okay when it's not, just to spare their feelings.

Caring about them with detachment means you care that they are unhappy, but you do not take on the responsibility to make them feel better and become whole again. You might be made to feel that you are the "problem," and since it's all your fault, it's on you to fix it. You alone cannot be responsible for any one person's feelings. Stay away from their mental distortions and stick to your boundary.

But What About When They Keep Pushing?

When they push back or have a negative reaction to your boundary, then you simply reiterate your boundary more firmly. It is crucially important that you don't rescind your boundary. You don't need to change or take back your boundary just because they don't like it. You simply need to reinforce it with a mixture of empathy, firmness, and detachment. Your statement might sound like this:

- I understand this might be hard for you to hear, but this isn't up for debate.

- I hear what you're saying [it can be helpful for you to paraphrase it back], but it doesn't change how I feel.

- My position won't change. I'm sorry if that upsets you; it's not my intention.

- I have already asked you to stop. Please respect my boundary.

- This conversation can't continue if you talk to me like that.

You might be thinking, *This sounds hard to pull off. Have you met my bitchy mother-in-law or my psychotic ex-husband?* I feel you. Reiterating your boundaries takes practice. In previous chapters we talked about visualizing physical separation to help shield you from your manipulator. An imaginary shield can be helpful in detaching yourself from the other person's reaction or from the fear of provoking them. Create the visual barrier that works for you during a discussion when you are feeling intimidated or overwhelmed. Here are some ideas to try:

- While conversing, you can imagine you are gently pressing the button to the side of your driver's-side seat in the car to raise an imaginary window between you and this person. You can picture a glass gate emerging between you or tuck yourself into your own imaginary bubble.

- As I mentioned before, my client who lives on a farm likes to imagine a beehive falling on her mother's head every time she yells at her. The buzzing sound of bumblebees soothes her.

- If you find the person intimidating, a helpful concept is to imagine you are talking to a small, naughty child. Or the small child version of this person. Or picture the person dressed in a clown suit or any image that can help diminish their intensity or stature.

But I'm Afraid of Their Anger . . .

Manipulators commonly use anger to control people, and caretakers often acquiesce, give in, surrender, and roll over just to avoid the other person's anger. Think about what you fear might happen if they get angry. Now think about how you might be able to handle that if it happens. For instance, you might worry that if you break up with him, he might tell everyone you know that you are a horrible person. Okay, what are the people who really know you, or know you both, likely to think? That you're horrible? Or that he's mad he got dumped? Another example is that he might show up on your porch and demand to see you. How might you deal with that? Call the police or threaten to call the police if he doesn't leave. Almost anything you imagine, except in cases of domestic violence, is something survivable, albeit uncomfortable.

Then There's Guilt . . . Mine

While you are setting boundaries and practicing detachment, guilt often worms its way into your brain. You might find yourself thinking, *Do I really need to be this harsh? Isn't this kind of mean? They are going to become extremely upset, all because of me.*

These thoughts are common guilt-provoking narratives your manipulator is feeding you implicitly or explicitly. He might accuse you of being disloyal. He might call you ice cold, cruel, or accuse you of lacking empathy. He might quietly sulk in front of you, hoping his sad-sack expression will haunt you badly enough to take back your boundaries and cheer him up again.

Often your own guilt is associated with some form of hope that maybe these boundaries aren't necessary. You might be hoping he will act right or treat you better, and then you won't have to ask for space or move out or stop doing whatever it is you're doing that he doesn't like.

My client Brenda waited until her son went off to college out of state before she swiftly moved out of the house, leaving her abusive husband of nineteen years with the dog and two goldfish. Every time she went over there to pick up the mail, he would sit on a chair and sulk. "Do you really have to do this?" he would mutter over and over, crying in his cup of coffee. He confessed to her that now that she's gone, he can't eat, sleep, or go to work. He also accused her of turning his son against him since he never calls or visits him. Perhaps it never occurred to him that his son knows what kind of prick his own dad is. Maybe her ex-husband is not the sharpest tool in the drawer in that regard, but I will say he deserves an award for playing the victim like a movie star. In a session with me, she reported that she would drive back home to her own little apartment, flooded with guilt, wondering, *Do I really have to do this to him?*

When I asked her again why she decided to leave him, she reminded me of all the abuse she'd endured. She replayed all the times he'd cheated on her with other women, while accusing her of cheating on him. He brazenly flirted with other women right in front of her, and then he would call her a whore if she so much as smiled at a handsome waiter. He often left her at home when he got invited to parties and social events, making himself laugh with his charming analogy, "as if I would bring a sandwich to a buffet."

On top of all the abuse, all the ways he gaslit her, and all the ways he projected everything onto her, he never once apologized for his cruel behavior. My response to her was, "It sounds to me, then, that you are not doing anything *to him*; what you are doing is for yourself. It only needs to make sense to you."

She trailed back to her guilt as she grappled with that tiny "what if" narrative that surfaces in moments of guilt. What if he could change? Let's see, what if he could change? Don't you think that within the span of nineteen years he would have changed already, or at least tried to change? Before or even after you left and filed for divorce? Has he even expressed a desire to change? No? Then what makes you think he will?

People who rescue other people get stuck in guilt all too easily. Guilt drives the behavior to rescue and take care of others because they lose sight of themselves as a separate entity. Instead of prioritizing your own self, you are rushing to the aid of others who claim you are the one, the only one, who can save them from their unbearable feelings. When really, the only one you need to save is yourself.

Stages of Detachment

Detaching essentially means letting go, and it can be processed in stages, similar to the stages of grief related to dying. While breakups, or distancing yourself, are not actual deaths, they are still losses you grieve as you are forced to accept that a relationship is not offering what it seemed to promise. A Swiss American psychiatrist named Elisabeth Kübler-Ross created the Kübler-Ross model to explain the constantly shifting, complicated grieving process. The five stages of grief are denial, anger, bargaining, depression, and acceptance, which take place in no specific chronological order. Each stage can occur and reoccur at any time as you cycle through the stages while you grieve your loss. Similarly, you might go through the same stages as you evaluate and consider ending a troubling relationship.

The denial stage happens as you cling to the belief or false hope that the other person will finally recognize your experience in this relationship and make the necessary changes. You continue to argue without success while you stay on this toxic merry-go-round of a relationship. You are rooted firmly in the denial stage as long as you continue to hope this person will change. In this stage, you are feeling stuck because you think you need this person to act differently and fail to think about the kinds of changes you could be making for yourself instead.

The anger stage usually happens once you have opened your eyes to the injustice you've been experiencing. Since caretakers usually feel weird about being angry themselves, you might get uncomfortable with this emotion when it comes up. The good news about the new feeling of anger is that you are now beginning to admit that there is a real problem. The cat's out of the bag, *me-fucking-ow*, and you are officially pissed off. Clients in this stage often apologize to me during therapy for popping off at the mouth with a sharp new attitude about this person. In such cases, I reassure them that this is progress. It's okay to be angry when you finally realize that you've been treated unfairly and you don't want to take it anymore. You go, girl!

At times, your anger will be directed at them and other times at yourself, for having put up with way too much bullshit for way too long. Since caretakers can't resist the urge to blame themselves, you might spend a good amount of time figuratively smacking yourself in the head over and over for letting this person into your life, ignoring the signs, or just putting up with their shit for so long. We will talk about self-forgiveness later, in part 4 of this book.

The bargaining stage is when you are no longer in denial and yet you are not ready to throw in the towel, so you focus on what you can do to recharge or repair the relationship. This might look like learning to communicate more effectively, setting boundaries perhaps for the first time, or managing your boundaries with more conviction. I fully endorse all these steps. It might also look like going on vacation together, threatening divorce, going to couples therapy, or maybe even having a child together with the naïve hope that this new human being will somehow bring you closer together, instead of realizing that you have just created a human to triangulate with later. (Some of these steps might work, but others might fail on an epic scale.) This stage is filled with the *what if* thoughts that keep you rooted in hope.

The depression stage happens when everything you have tried has failed. Hope has been replaced by an unsettling reality. If you are in the grips of a narcissist, you are dealing with someone who is incapable of self-reflection, empathy, or mutual understanding. You feel utterly defeated and drained, and feelings of depression are triggered. Maybe your friends are sick of hearing about your prick boyfriend or maybe your couples' therapist fired you. You know the relationship is not going to get any better. It's sinking lower and lower each day that goes by, like a ship with a giant hole in the bottom.

Fortunately, the depression stage indicates an awareness that there is nothing you can do to save this relationship. This stage is often plagued with the notion that all the years you've invested in this person have gone to waste. You imagined a different life for yourself. Maybe you had dreams of starting a family, and the thought of starting all over again with a hypothetical partner feels totally depressing or unimaginable. What you are grieving is the life you could have had but don't have anymore. Often, the grief is associated with the loss of the life you imagined, not the actual person.

The acceptance stage connects you with the idea that your powerlessness in changing this person is actually a relief. You can stop trying to fix, change, control, rescue, cure, caretake, or do whatever crazy shit you've been trying to do with this person without success.

You are ready to get off the merry-go-round. This realization can feel calming in some way, as you no longer have to participate in their insanity. The shit show is over, folks; take the rest of your popcorn and go home.

Understanding the stages of grief is a way to help you make sense of the roller coaster of feelings you might be experiencing as you process an unhealthy relationship.

Hope

Hope can keep co-dependency alive. Hope that he might change. Hope that you can change, fix, or rescue him. Is it hope or false hope? Consider how realistic your hope is. False hope usually involves a special "if only" track playing in your head that disconnects you from reality. If only he would (blank), then (blank). See how all these *if only* statements keep you invested in an unrealistic future.

If only...	Then...	The Reality
He would stop drinking.	Everything would be great.	If he is not committed to or interested in recovery, then you are not about to find out.
He would marry me.	These problems would go away.	There is no guarantee that a bigger commitment will erase your current issues. In fact, they tend to worsen.
He could control his temper.	We would never fight.	Is he taking an anger management course? Is he going to therapy? No? Then you will keep fighting.
He would stop flirting with other women.	I would be happy in the relationship.	What you are actually saying is, if only he would respect me, I would be happy.

Hang In or Bail Out

Tory, an athletic woman in her early thirties, bustled into the room on her first session sporting matching activewear and a big smile. Her cheeriness began to fade as she delved into the story of her disappointing relationship with Brandon who, after two years together, still refused to talk about marriage. He "wasn't ready" to move in together, and talks of marriage were left vague. *If only I knew where this relationship was headed*, she often thought.

"All he wants to do after work is sit at home, smoke weed, eat buffalo wings, and watch TV," she complained. "I wish we could be more active together, like waking up early Sunday mornings to go on a hike! Or maybe a bike ride on the beach. I keep suggesting a trip to Hawaii or Mexico, but he just rolls his eyes and says he's happy where he is."

Wow, Brandon sounds like a blast. Each session for weeks focused on the ways Brandon was letting her down. She took notes when we discussed effective communication strategies, hoping they might work on her stoned, shut-in boyfriend. She tried desperately to draw him out of his shell. Tory was determined to find out whether Brandon was ever going to ask her to marry him.

Finally, I asked Tory this question: What would we be focusing on here today if we weren't talking about Brandon? She reflected on that with me, and her responses surprised her. We talked about what she could be doing instead, which is already a great start. "Well, I would probably go to the gym more," she answered. "And I've always wanted to try hot yoga, but he won't go with me." I asked her what keeps her from going by herself. "I don't know. I usually spend most evenings with him when I get off work." We talked about how it would feel to sign up for yoga and just start going. How it would feel to start living her life, instead of waiting around for a pothead to adopt healthier habits and finally ask her to marry him.

Focusing on herself allowed her to gradually regain her confidence. She began to see on her own that this relationship wasn't meeting her needs, that her lifestyle was not compatible with Brandon's, and that these factors were unlikely to change. Confidence, along with self-awareness, helps you see your relationship more clearly because your lens isn't clouded with fear. Fear colors so much of our decision-making. I have listened to Tory and so many more clients admit that the main reason they don't end a toxic or unsatisfying relationship is the fear of being alone. They wonder if putting up with the dickhead they know still beats being alone.

Learning to prioritize yourself despite the fear of being alone allows you to build the confidence necessary to overcome that fear. Confidence strips away the fear of being alone for at least two reasons: (1) the idea of being alone forever is not realistic when you know your worth, and (2) being alone isn't so bad when you value yourself and realize being on your own means you have options.

Ultimately, confidence gives you the clarity and the courage to leave a relationship that is not meeting your needs. You need to be cool with being alone before you can merge lives with someone else in a healthy way. You should be out there living your best life, and then you might meet someone who adds more to your already happy existence. Otherwise, you're hoping some lame asshole will come along and fill a void. That scenario has proven to never work well for anyone. If the fear of being alone is what is tethering you to someone, I suggest you start imagining how your life could look without this person and how you could embrace being alone for some period of time. Being alone today doesn't mean your destiny is to grow into a lonely, withered old hag who talks to herself all day while sitting in a rocking chair. Your single status is just a moment in time, regardless of your current age.

Being single brings you much closer to finding a happy relationship than staying with someone who doesn't make you happy because you need to free yourself from the constraints of that relationship before you can meet someone new. Even more than that, while you are putting all this energy toward someone who is not good for you, it is taking a toll on you and crushing your spirit, which keeps you stuck. You will not get rewarded by the universe while you're sitting on the ground accepting crumbs.

I've heard clients fret about getting too old to break up with someone. *But I have put in so much time with this person. I would hate to think of all the years I have wasted.* Well, how many more years do you want to waste? If the relationship is not getting better, then you are *still wasting your years.* Sometimes you have to know when to cut your losses. And besides, when you think about it, letting go of someone who doesn't respect you, value you, or appreciate you is not a loss at all; it's a gain. Think about everything you have to gain when you let go of someone who is keeping you from finding a healthier and more fulfilling relationship. Think about everything you have to gain when you free up the space they are taking. If they are not giving you what you want in a partnership, they are a placeholder, not a partner.

Shifting from Caretaking to Self-Care

There is an irony to co-dependency that becomes apparent when you examine your relational patterns. If you are co-dependent, you might appear strong when you really feel powerless. You might be accused of trying to control someone when in reality you are allowing yourself to be controlled by their moods, disorders, addictions, and behaviors. You might think you are trying to help people whereas you actually feel helpless yourself as you become enslaved to your perception and anticipation of their needs.

If reading this gave you an aha moment of sorts, then practicing detachment is your recovery solution. It doesn't mean you necessarily have to end certain relationships and cut off all contact with certain people. Practicing healthy detachment will help you evaluate when it might become necessary or feel better to make that call. More specifically, as you practice healthy boundaries and learn to stop over-extending yourself to rescue people who elicit that response in you, you will find that some people appreciate your honesty and accept your boundaries. Those relationships have a chance to grow and improve. If, on the flip side, you find that certain people are not respecting your new boundaries, then you will need to increase the firmness of your boundaries. If that doesn't work, at a certain point, your healthy detachment from their reaction to your boundaries is what will help you make the decision to end a relationship that feels imbalanced, exhausting, and infinitely focused on their needs and desires.

When you are taking care of yourself instead of other people, that is when you will know for yourself which relationships feel right and which ones you are better off letting go of. Essentially, you learn to do what you have to do to protect yourself.

Remember that the people who don't respect your boundaries are the ones who were benefiting greatly from your lack of boundaries in the first place. Sitting with that thought for a moment might shed some light on the specific individuals who might be taking advantage of you. And maybe they don't ever want to stop taking advantage of you because, let's face it, that bountiful gravy train has been too good to them. Why should they stop now? You have been conditioning them to get goodies from you over and over again for who knows how long, so it is going to take some slow untangling to reverse a dynamic they have been benefiting from. This process requires consistency and a ton of patience. Ultimately, you get to decide when your patience runs out and when it's time to choose yourself over a person who doesn't understand what your needs are and maybe doesn't even care about your needs. You can't understand it for them. You can say it over and over, and what they understand is ultimately up to them.

Since you can't change the other person, it will be *your* change in behavior that tests the potential of the relationship. Your change, not theirs, will help you see the relationship for what it is and what the relationship is capable of. This will let you make the right decision for yourself, without letting the fear of loneliness stand in your way.

Detaching with Love and Firmness

If you identify with the caretaker and co-dependent patterns, learning to detach can feel particularly challenging. Detachment is considered a core component of co-dependent recovery. The following are some general guidelines and principles to follow as you learn to detach with love and firmness, reversing your caretaker impulses to more appropriate and balanced self-care.

First, focus on what you can control and what you cannot. In Alcoholics Anonymous meetings and Al-Anon meetings, the serenity prayer is often chanted by the group at the end: *I learn to accept the things I cannot change, have the courage to change the things that I can, and the wisdom to know the difference.*

This phrase is powerful because it reinforces the idea that you can only change what you have direct control over, and generally speaking, the only thing you are guaranteed to have control over is yourself. You cannot control anybody else. It's important to learn the difference and learn to let go of trying so hard to change or control others.

Sometimes this involves letting other people make their own decisions, good or bad. Yes, it means letting your buddy step in a shit puddle. Not literally, of course. Let your friends and loved ones make their own mistakes and learn from them on their own. Give advice when asked, but resist the urge to give unsolicited advice.

Remind yourself of what doesn't feel right about a relationship or interaction, and then give yourself permission to feel that. Next, speak up about what you are feeling or what you might need, regardless of whether it aligns with the others person's needs. Be clear about what you need.

Notice when you are obsessing over someone else's problems. And then quit obsessing over other people's problems. Don't take responsibility for other people's behavior or the results of their choices.

Pay attention to when you are working harder to solve another person's problem or help them than they are. Support is great; you are supporting people when they are helping themselves. When they aren't helping themselves, your help is not support; it's unhealthy caretaking and rescuing. Don't help people more than they are helping themselves.

Learn to respond instead of reacting or overreacting. Step back from the situation and think about what you want to say, and then consider the impact of that message. Make sure to respond when you are calm after you've had time to reflect.

Try new responses that are different from your more emotional ones. Imagine how different it might feel to not take some things so personally. Maybe you can try to ignore some minuscule issue that would normally fluster you or send you over the edge. See how it feels to choose a different response.

Exit, leave the room, hang up, or silence your device if you can't control your reactions or if the person in front of you can't either.

Ask for what you need. Speak up! Set your boundaries and maintain your boundaries, without wavering. Make sure your expectations of others are realistic so your unrealistic expectations don't fill you with resentment.

Remember this:

You have to be ready to walk away from any deal if you want to get the best deal.

PART FOUR

Your New Life

Chapter 12

YOUR MINDSET: BUILDING YOUR CONFIDENCE

I HAVE ALWAYS BEEN AFRAID TO CHECK my luggage when I travel, fearing that some hooligan will steal it and I'll never again see my favorite indispensable items that I take with me everywhere. Paranoid or not, I always remain vigilant in the baggage claim area when waiting to reunite with my checked luggage.

One time, I arrived from a tropical vacation at midnight and stood in the baggage claim area where suitcases swirled before the exhausted travelers. Remaining as vigilant as ever, I noticed my unique rose-gold metallic suitcase drop onto the conveyer belt. Next, I noticed a man confidently pluck my suitcase and walk off with it. He glided with my unique suitcase over to a young woman, and together they began their exit through automatic double doors. My stomach dropped as I evaluated the odds of my suitcase's twin making an appearance on the same flight. As the couple was dragging what could only be my suitcase along the sidewalk to the parking structure, I instinctively lurched after them. I figured there would be no harm in inquiring. I had no idea what to expect as I scrambled after alleged thieves in the airport.

I finally caught up to them. "I happen to have a suitcase exactly like that one! Let's check the tags, shall we?" I spoke in a polite, self-assured tone. The woman immediately pushed my suitcase toward me. "It's yours," she said, backing away apologetically. The man did nothing; he just stood there with his mouth open.

Not only did it turn out to be the easiest confrontation ever, but it was also successful. I was instantly reunited with my almost-stolen belongings and went on my merry way. It was successful because, in that split second, I deemed myself important enough to initiate the confrontation. I didn't back away from what I was convinced belonged to me, and on the rare chance it might not be mine, I didn't care what I might have looked like running after my suitcase's clone. When you give yourself permission to be important, you are less likely to become a victim in someone else's plot.

Confident people are less likely to be targets for manipulation and abuse. Your confidence is an automatic shield that discourages manipulators. Earlier chapters in this book have already presented you with some confidence-building tools. You might recall from chapter 6 on the Bully how to position yourself with confidence and stand like a Chesty Peacock as a way to shield yourself from bullies since they are looking for weak people with low self-esteem. Your confidence will protect you from any type of predator or manipulator because it convinces them you are not fuck-with-able.

In any self-defense class or martial art, including Brazilian jiu-jitsu, you will learn that your posture is your first line of self-defense. Standing tall and straight, walking with purpose, remaining aware of your surroundings at all times is discouraging to predators. It tells them you won't be an easy target and therefore are not worth the trouble. You might fight back, cause a scene, and generally become the kind of nuisance they regret bothering with. Think about interpersonal relationships the same way. Just like a boot always wants to land on a nice doormat, so do emotional predators and manipulators.

If you believe you lack confidence, it might be one of the reasons you got yourself stuck with a manipulator in the first place. Or perhaps this toxic person gradually over time siphoned all the confidence you ever had right out of you. Or a combination of both. Getting gaslit over and over while you scramble to save the confusing relationship you've been drowning in has undoubtedly diminished your confidence.

The following are some of the actions confident people take that you can start doing today.

Owning Your Voice

When you consider that confidence comes from knowing who you are and standing up for your core beliefs, you can see how important your own self-awareness is. Pay attention to how you truly think and feel, and then be ready to manage your boundaries with unwavering conviction. Consider what is negotiable and what isn't. And then stand by what isn't, giving zero fucks about whoever doesn't like it. That is confidence and courage, something manipulators don't want to mess with.

Whether you feel like you are inherently an assertive person or not, try stepping into the role of assertiveness anyway. Try this persona on and start asserting yourself by setting boundaries, as discussed in chapter 10. Notice the shift. When you behave with assertiveness, you become assertive, and then you feel more assertive over time because you notice what it does for you. Assertiveness becomes positively reinforced each time you try it with success. This is how you grow your confidence, by acting with confidence and then genuinely feeling the confidence inside you as you step into that role of a confident person.

I worked on assertiveness training with Brie, who was living with her narcissistic girlfriend. At first, she didn't want to leave her because she truly hoped she might change. But their relational cycle was on repeat and was unlikely to produce any kind of change. We talked about how she could not control how her girlfriend behaved, but she could consider how *she* could behave differently. We discussed what part she could play in the change she desired. I recommended she start standing up to her and see what happens. As she began to set boundaries and step into a more assertive role, things got worse; her girlfriend became even more angry and manipulative. She reported that she began acting like a bratty child throwing a tantrum, and for the first time, Brie was totally turned off by her. She no longer felt like trying to please her or calm her down. She began to look down on her, felt repulsed by her, and finally wanted to leave. Empowering yourself gives you confidence, and confidence changes your perception of everything, including how you see others. She broke up with her after that. Today, a year later, she is in a happy, new relationship with someone else, living her best life.

While you are trying on assertiveness, pay attention to the manipulator's intimidation tactics. Brie's girlfriend threw childish tantrums, but as you are well aware by now, there are tons of tricks they might try. If they try to overpower you by shouting over your words, simply disengage without giving up your position on the matter. Remain silently in control by holding true to your opinions or knowing your course of action in the face of their protest. If they make threats about what might happen, don't let them rattle you. Consider taking their threats with a tiny grain of salt. Evaluate whether they are likely to follow through with their threat, and even if they were to follow through, consider the impact it would really have on you. It is usually not as scary as it sounds.

For instance, manipulators enjoy tossing around lawsuit threats. Often there is no legal case, and even if there were, they are not likely to spend the money, time, and energy to follow through for little to no gain. The threat is often merely a scare tactic. They also love their smear campaigns and might threaten to drag your name through the dirt or tell people a ridiculously distorted narrative about you. Let them. They probably won't. And even if they do, consider the impact it will have on you. People who know you will catch on quickly, and the friendships you lose as a result were probably not that solid in the first place. Try to see it this way—you just got help weeding out the dumb or disloyal ones.

Trusting Your Gut

How many times have you kicked yourself, thinking, *I knew I shouldn't have done that*. Yet, you did it anyway. Why? Because humans talk themselves out of their intuitive voice all the time. We'll take advice from our high-before-noon cousin or our nosy neighbor down the street before we listen to our own intuition. We contradict ourselves with logic and reason, ignoring our own precious instincts that are meant to guide us.

Our minds are often swirling with a confusing combination of instinct, logic, and fear, making it extremely difficult to decipher which voice is our own intuition. If you're not sure what you're listening to half the time in your noisy head, you are not alone. Many people freak out when it's time to make a decision because they are overwhelmed by all the chatter in their mind. One way to decipher which thought is your intuition is by understanding that it is often the first thought that comes to you.

The root of the word intuition means to guard or protect. Your intuition is meant to guide and protect you. In his book *The Gift of Fear*, author Gavin de Becker, who praises intuition as the cornerstone of safety, explains the way humans often dismiss their own intuition while giving more merit to conscious thought and logic. "Intuition is soaring flight compared to the plodding of logic," he argues, maintaining that the human brain is most efficient and invested when its host is at risk, which catapults our intuition to a whole new level. He describes scenarios in which people who were in violent danger trusted and relied on something in their gut, and it is precisely that intuition that ended up saving their life. While murder is obviously more extreme and dramatic than emotional abuse, the predatory process is the same. Stop second-guessing yourself. Every victim of lethal violence who argued "but he seems so nice" or "well, I don't want to be rude" ended up dead.

Cutting Through the Bullshit

In addition to noticing their intimidation tactics, it really helps to stop taking things so damn personally. First of all, narcissists and toxic people say a lot of crazy shit. Most of the shit that comes out of their mouth is a reflection of them and what they desperately need to believe, more than it is about you. You cannot let yourself get worked up over all the little shit they have to say because that is how they keep manipulating you. As long as you agree to enslave yourself to their reality, they continue to control and manipulate you. Remember that something is not necessarily true just because some asshole said it. You don't even need to argue with them. Just leave their bullshit alone.

Imagine you are walking through the streets of Paris on your glorious vacation one crisp autumn afternoon. The smell of fresh crepes is wafting through the breeze. Orange and caramel-colored leaves have fallen to the ground like cheerful confetti when suddenly you stumble across a pile of dog shit on the sidewalk. Now, you can stand there and hysterically protest how unfair and rotten it is that someone would litter the beautiful streets of Paris with a bold pile of their dog's unremoved fecal matter, or you can simply step over it with a sideways wince, refusing to let it spoil the rest of your perfect day. I think we can all agree that the latter and not the former is the way to go here.

Confidence is the ability to rise above anything that smells like bullshit. When you fully understand that their bullshit is just that— their bullshit and not yours, they lose their credibility and sense of importance. Consider the source anytime someone makes a diminishing or hurtful remark about you. If this person is ego-driven or manipulative, you can somewhat safely assume that much of what they say is bullshit and choose to rise above it.

Whether your manipulator is cutting you down, telling a persuasive lie, trying to trick you, or trying to spook you, they're most likely just talking shit, which means you don't have to believe it, argue against it, clear it up, or let it take up any of your energy. Simply rise above it. You don't need to subscribe to their bullshit anymore. Cancel your subscription.

Ignoring bullshit is the perfect segue to the next topic.

Start Giving Out Less Fucks

In his book *The Subtle Art of Not Giving a F*ck*, author Mark Manson says, "In my life, I have given a fuck about many things. I have also *not* given a fuck about many things. And like the road not taken, it was the fucks not given that made all the difference." What the man is saying, folks, is choose your fucks wisely. If you let yourself give a fuck about every wild hair that tickles your butt crack, you are losing sight of what is important. Getting caught up in all the trivial nonsense that life has to offer keeps you frustrated and unfulfilled, and for what? Reserve your fucks for something truly meaningful and productive. When you remain connected to your goals, your values, and your life purpose, you are an unstoppable force.

Staying connected to your goals, values, and life purpose also means giving zero fucks about what others think of you. In this book, we have talked a lot about staying out of people's heads. What other people think of you is none of your business because it has more to do with them—their taste, their hang-ups, their personal history, their trauma, their personality, their genetic wiring, thousands of things about them—and little or nothing to do with you.

Confident people are confident *not* because they invariably believe everyone in the universe likes them. They are confident because they literally don't give a fuck if someone does or doesn't. Not in a socio-pathic way, but in a self-assured way. Also, confident people understand the world is subjective and you cannot universally please everyone. Every literary masterpiece ever written has a critic who didn't like it. Every hit song ever recorded has someone who hates it and will instantly skip over it on their playlist. Have you ever laughed your ass off watching your favorite comedy while the person next to you didn't get it and wanted to watch something else? Human beings are not the same. Not everyone will get you, and that's okay, because the right ones will. Let go of what others think of you while you continue to do you.

Remember that you are only responsible for your own words, actions, and choices, not other people's reactions to them. You don't need everyone's approval for every move you make. When manipulative people try to convince you that you have done something wrong, and you know with every fiber of your being that your intentions are pure, it is not your job to set them straight after you have explained it the first time. Let them freak out about whatever they want to freak out about, and keep going about your business.

Now, while you are not giving a fuck what others think of you, that doesn't mean to shut out all constructive criticism and personal feedback. Confidence also means being able to absorb outside, con-flicting information with an open mind. When you receive information about yourself, consider how this information can be helpful to you and to people around you. Consider the source—does this person appear to be looking out for me and my best interest? Consider the truthfulness—is there any possible truth or accuracy to this? If so, how can I use this information to my advantage? How can I use this information to improve myself or help others? Try to reflect on feedback you are given without taking it so damn personally.

Grow Your Own Grass (and Don't Worry about Anyone Else's)

I'm not talking about growing your own weed. Or I guess I could be—if you're actually growing a marijuana plant in your bathtub, then by all means, have at it. I'm referring to the idea that the grass is not always greener somewhere else; it's greenest where it's nurtured. Tend to your own grass or whatever your pursuit is, and don't give even the tiniest hairy rat's ass about what anyone else is doing. Quit looking around and worrying about who might be ahead of you, and keep going on your own unique path.

Do not ever compare yourself to other people. There will always be someone hotter, cuter, richer, thinner, fitter, younger, smarter, faster, more talented, or better in some way. It is inevitable and a complete waste of time and energy to spend one precious minute thinking about what someone else has going on. Comparison is a surefire way to zap all the joy and inspiration right out of your life.

Think of how dull the world would be if every person who wanted to do something stopped and worried about who else was doing it too. What if a foodie entrepreneur with his flight of colorful margaritas wanted to open a Mexican restaurant but stopped in front of a popular taco truck and said, *They're already selling tacos around here; there goes my Mexican cantina idea.* Or, if Mario came to Los Angeles from Naples and said, *Oh there are already a lot of pizzerias here, they probably don't need one more.* Are you kidding? Our favorite pizza place literally wouldn't exist if that is how Mario from Naples thought. Janet Jackson didn't sit down and say, *My brother Michael is already a famous pop star; he has a special white glove and everything. I should just give up and do something else with my life.* Nope, Ms. Jackson went on and did her Janet thang, and then became one of the most influential female pop singers of the '80s and '90s with a ton of hit singles.

Buyer versus Seller Mentality

My clients often ask me how to feel less socially anxious and awkward in social settings. Marlene said every time she meets people she becomes gripped with fear and anxiety over how others will perceive her. She feels so nervous that not only is she convinced she is making a horrible first impression, but also the entire experience ends up sucking giant donkey dicks and makes her never want to socialize again.

This is what I told Marlene and all the others. The problem is that you are walking into these situations as the seller, not the buyer, and you have to reverse that. *Say what?* Imagine you are walking into a car dealership that has dozens of cars to look at or test drive. While you are strolling around, as the buyer, you are thinking about what these cars have to offer. You are thinking about what makes this car interesting and whether you want to spend more time with this car or move on to another car. Even if you walked up to the only car on the lot and there were no other cars, as the buyer, you would be showing curiosity in the car and asking the seller questions about the car to see whether this particular car works for you. You would have little to no interest in what the seller thinks of you.

This is exactly how you should approach social situations. As the buyer, you are not selling yourself to this person, presenting all your

positive attributes, hoping they will like you. Instead, you are showing curiosity in the other person, learning about them and how they
might contribute to your experience. You should be thinking about
what this person has to offer you, instead of what you have to offer
them. Ask people questions and try to find out what makes them
interesting to talk to while you are in the same room together. While
you are doing so, pay attention to how this person makes you feel.
Do you feel good vibes, or does something in your gut make you
want to run for the hills just to get away from this person? Chances
are, when a person creates a negative experience by merely talking
about themselves, they are probably toxic or unhealthy in some way.

I met a guy at a small gathering once. I noticed that throughout
our entire encounter, he kept staring straight over my head. He rattled off some of his favorite movie titles that he believed everyone
should watch, without asking about anyone else's interest in films.
In an effort to stay engaged, I commented on his favorites list and
suggested similar ones he might enjoy with his obvious affinity for
dystopian futuristic dramas. Meanwhile, he kept staring straight over
my head with a deadpan expression, continuing to tell us all what we
should watch. I could have yawned or set myself on fire and this guy
wouldn't have noticed. Later, the host informed me that the guy was
the arrogant, hothead neighbor next door who gets invited to their
parties as a preemptive strategy to avoid noise complaints, and not
to take his rudeness personally. Luckily, I didn't. And neither should
you if someone ever behaves in a strange manner and does not put you
at ease, for any reason at all.

Focusing on the other person instead of yourself takes away the
pressure and preoccupation with yourself. You stop anxiously performing. Instead, you begin to naturally present yourself as curious and
interesting by showing interest in someone else. Interesting people are
interested in *others*, in other people and other things, not themselves.

Your Mental Diet

We can't leave affirmations and positive self-talk out of a chapter on confidence, although a lot of stuff out there on positive self-affirmations is super cheesy. I'm sure you've been told to look at yourself in the mirror and tell yourself, "I am beautiful" and "I am worth it," which might feel more like you are auditioning for a L'Oréal commercial than anything else. Also, if you don't believe any of that stuff in the first place, it might feel fake and pointless.

What feels important for you to believe about yourself? If you are still struggling to believe important things about yourself, think about someone who loves you and admires you. It could be your mom, your boyfriend, your best friend, your coolest aunt, whomever. Now, try to see what they see. If you're not sure, ask them. And then see yourself through their eyes. Not your critical eyes, but their eyes.

The negative crap you've been feeding yourself has a bigger impact on you than you might realize. Consider where your negative self-talk has been coming from. A critical parent? A toxic ex-partner? Some asshole in the subway station? Sometimes the way you trash talk yourself is simply someone else's voice that got stuck in your brain. When you identify whose voice that is, consider the source, as discussed earlier in "Cutting Through the Bullshit," and remember, this is their bullshit, not yours. Dismiss this negative information about yourself as invalid and instead give more credibility to the supportive, loving people who are rooting for you.

If you want an affirmation exercise that might feel more productive than the L'Oréal commercial, try this: Maybe you've seen nutrition articles suggesting you replace your junk food with a healthy alternative, such as, *Don't Eat: French Fries / Eat Instead: Baked Carrot Strings!* Let's do the same thing with your thoughts. Make a list of your junk food thoughts, and replace them with healthier thoughts about yourself using the affirmation that suits you specifically. Here are some examples.

Don't think:	Think instead:	And also:
I'm not good enough.	It is not possible to make everyone happy all the time.	Here are some positive things about me . . .
I'm fat.	If I feel out of shape, I can set a goal to lose some weight.	I have athletic legs or great skin or amazing hair or a perfect belly button (just pick one positive thing to focus on).
I will never be successful.	I'm feeling stuck, so I need to revisit my goals or create an action plan so I can find the success I want.	Here are some things I have achieved, however small, even if I still want to achieve more things.

Quit Your Guilt Tripping

Guilt and shame are cock-blocking your very important relationship with yourself. Confidence requires being honest, gentle, and compassionate with yourself. You cannot go back in time and undo what is done. There's no point in smacking yourself on the head over and over for spending too much money on Amazon, gaining fifteen pounds, or trusting that dirtbag you met on Tinder. All you can do is examine your mistakes, seek to understand them, learn from them, and create the kind of change that will benefit your life.

Your own unnecessary guilt trips can get in the way, though. What is guilt and why do we do that to ourselves? Guilt is defined as feeling remorse for an offense or wrongdoing, whether real or imagined. Then there's guilt's nasty cousin, shame, the painful, often intolerable awareness of one's own character defects. Guilt is about the act, whereas shame is about the unbearably flawed self. For some, guilt and shame blend together without distinction. Shame can be toxic and paralyzing and can send us messages about our worthlessness. Shame often comes from failing to live up to the expectations imposed on you by your family, society, or even yourself.

Narcissists are not unique in suppressing their shame. Avoiding shame can become a lifetime pursuit for many people. People will sometimes find escape routes in drug and alcohol abuse to numb their feelings of inferiority, anxiety, or worthlessness. This self-medication strategy temporarily keeps them from examining their perceived character defects, but it cannot be sustained without long-term self-destructive effects on their lives. Others will elude triggers of shame with bursts of anger and rage, which provide powerful distractions from their feelings while also damaging their relationships. Shame can also surface a tough inner critic that demands unrealistic standards of perfectionism, which generates anxiety about failing to meet those standards, creating a self-perpetuating cycle of shame and negativity. As you can see, none of these coping mechanisms serve as effective solutions for moving beyond shame in a healthy way.

Try to pinpoint which expectations you have imposed on yourself and how they are serving you. Allowing your self-worth to be determined by unrealistic markers, perfect standards, and idealized versions of yourself creates the basis for shame. Everyone's journey is different and unique, so if you embrace the expectations that serve *you* without comparison and judgment, you can extinguish the shame holding you hostage. People say things like, "I should get married by the time I'm thirty" or "I should own a house instead of renting this crappy apartment." Imagine how liberating it would feel to simply remove the "should" statements.

Moving beyond shame requires you to listen to your inner thoughts without judgment. If you are calling yourself a giant loser for one reason or another, where does this voice come from? Is this your mom or dad's voice? Or your sibling's voice? Maybe your hothead gym coach in elementary school? I don't know whose voice got stuck in your head, but the point is, it might not be your voice at all, and you don't need to listen to this voice. Once you examine where this might come from, you get to decide whether these are thoughts you want to keep or discard.

Our values and goals can shift throughout the course of our lives. Sometimes we adopt the values we were raised with, tackling goals we were encouraged to pursue and upholding beliefs we were told were the right ones. If that same value system still works for you, awesome, do not compromise it for anyone. If you find, however, that some of your philosophies are shifting, don't be afraid to try what feels right for you. If everyone in your family is a lawyer, but the thought of going to law school is a big snooze fest, then facing your parents' potential disappointment that you are not going to become their mini-me is way more important than giving up your dream to become a lion tamer, if that's what you truly want.

As you practice extending deeper compassion toward yourself, recognize that all human beings have character defects. All human beings disappoint other human beings. All human beings will screw up and step in shit at some point in their lives. Learn to self-soothe in response to your negative feelings, the same way you might soothe a scared child or a close friend. People tend to be more compassionate toward others than they are to themselves, so consider how much compassion you have to spare when you are observing your own thoughts and feelings. Basically, quit shit talking yourself and instead speak to yourself the same way you would to your stressed-the-fuck-out best friend.

Processing guilt and discarding shame is how you will learn to accept and love yourself. As you free yourself from the expectations imposed on you by society, your community, your family, and even your most critical self, your confidence will soar. Once you truly accept who you are in a solid, grounded way, nobody can shake that, no matter how powerful they are. Think about how difficult it is to manipulate a person who does not need your approval. That is the person you become when you genuinely accept and love yourself.

Forgiveness Is for You, Not Them

I have one more note on kicking shame in the ass and staunchly loving yourself. One of the paths to self-love is forgiveness all around. The most important person you will ever need to forgive is yourself. Forgiving yourself for whatever dumb-shit decisions you might have made in your lifetime (we've all made them) allows you to move beyond shame and truly accept yourself for all that you are.

Staying in a relationship with a lying, cheating fuckboy for too long doesn't mean there is anything wrong with you. All it means is that you didn't know what you know until you knew it. It means you left him when you were ready to leave him, however long it took to get to that point. And if you're kicking yourself for wasting your most youthful years on a scumbag, stop that. The scumbag was part of your unique, important journey, for whatever reason. You learned from that relationship, and you have more good years ahead. Trust me, you are not the first and only person on the planet to believe you have royally messed up some part of your life. You might have messed up, and guess what, you will mess up again. But if you learn from your messes, then you are on the path of self-improvement, where things will perk up.

Sometimes too, you will have to forgive the asshole—not necessarily because they deserve your forgiveness, but because you deserve relief and peace. Forgiving someone, whether you ever receive an apology or not, releases your own anger and resentment. Holding onto anger and resentment leads to feelings of depression and anxiety. Observational studies suggest that practicing forgiveness is related to lower levels of depression, anxiety, and hostility; reduced substance abuse; higher self-esteem; and greater life satisfaction. Forgiveness doesn't mean you forget what they did; it means you let go, refuse to let it consume you, and maybe stop fantasizing about them getting thrown out of a ten-story window.

Learn to Kick Some Ass, Literally!

I tell everyone I know that they should take martial arts or self-defense classes if they struggle with confidence, feel vulnerable to predators, or don't like walking alone to their car at night. Martial arts can be empowering because they teach you to carry yourself with confidence and poise. Learning how to fight back physically translates into a mindset that you carry with you psychologically. It gives you a feeling of safety in your body and comfort in your skin. Just knowing you are prepared to defend yourself generates confidence, whether you ever have to use what you learned or not. Basically, it gives you that *I'm a badass* feeling.

Remember this:

"Do not waste your precious time giving one single crap about what anyone else thinks of you," as shouted in all caps by Jen Sincero, the pioneer of Badassery, best-selling author, and success coach.[2]

---

2   Jen Sincero, *You're a Badass: How to Stop Doubting Your Greatness and Start Living an Awesome Life* (New York: Running Press, 2013), 64.

Chapter 13

YOUR NETWORK: MAKING THE RIGHT CONNECTIONS

BY NOW, YOU ARE PROBABLY FEELING more clarity regarding which people you want to either distance yourself from or ditch entirely. But what about the people you want to bring into your life and surround yourself with? Who you surround yourself with sets the tone for the life you will live.

Hanging out with the Negative Nancys and Debbie Downers means your time is spent listening to them relentlessly whine about how "life is so unfair." This will drown you so deep in negativity that staying afloat will only be that much harder. Make a conscious effort to avoid self-pity parties and people who love to shit on other people's parades.

Instead, stick with people who are positive, uplifting, and rooting for you. Confide in your honest friends and family members who have your back and will also give you their honest opinion. Hang out with people who are inspired, optimistic, enthusiastic, and believe the world is what you make it. If you don't know anyone like this, then you might need to make some new friends. Join activities, clubs, events, and groups that attract fun, positive, like-minded people who aren't whiney bitches.

The Bitch versus the Brutally Honest Real Friend

One of my best friends is a makeup artist who won't hesitate to ask me when I last exfoliated or point out that my eyebrows are starting to look like Spock from *Star Trek*. I've known her since middle school, and she has always been brutally honest. This is the kind of friend who will tell you when you have a scrap of lettuce decorating your front tooth at brunch, and she will never keep it to herself when she is suspicious of your new boyfriend. If this friend tells you she thinks your date is a loser or an asshole, it might sound bitchy, but pay attention. These are the kinds of friends who have your back. They are the truth tellers. We might not always like the truth they tell, but in a world full of yes-men telling us what we want to hear, we need more friends like this, or at least one friend like this.

Then there is the bitch. You will know the difference between the bitch and the brutally honest friend because the bitch is the same friend who tries to constantly one-up you. This is the kind of person who puts other people down in order to feel like the Top Banana or some kind of superstar at all times. As we've learned, the hothead with a superiority complex is actually a fragile ego that inflates itself by deflating others. Their unnecessary, and sometimes cruel, criticism comes from a need to squash their exaggerated shame of real or imagined inferiority. They will, of course, deny any trace of envy to maintain their coveted superior position. You might notice this friend becomes nicest to you when you are in a low place, crawling out of your ditch of despair, because she can continue to feel superior while offering a helpful hand. But if she doesn't cheer when you win or celebrate your success, watch out for that one. You might instinctively feel like this friend is not really in your corner, and if so, distance yourself or ditch that one altogether because you don't need friends like that.

Do Your Thang

First, you must be comfortable with yourself, on your own, doing what you love. Personal fulfillment is the biggest magnet to attracting other people. If you are looking to meet new people, whether you want more friends, Friday-night dates, or a special someone, first, *do your thang*, and then see what happens. People are attracted to other people who are living their best life doing what makes them happy.

For instance, if you absolutely love to dance but haven't gone out dancing since your senior prom many moons ago, then go frickin' dance already! Find a dance class or jump into the cardio booty shaker class (or whatever it's called) at your gym or just go out dancing! Some places offer dance lessons before the dancing starts, which is a great way to meet people. If you show up at one of these things alone, you won't be the only one. These places tend to be packed with everything from professional dancers who don't ever stop dancing to the sweaty-palmed, nervous, nice guy who is also eager to meet people. Don't write off that nervous dude; he might be hilarious once you get to know him.

Whatever your thing is, go find it and do it. You can literally find anything and everything these days. You can take art classes, even classes where you combine painting with drinking wine. Go play pickleball. Join a kickball league. Honestly, you don't even need to be athletic; if you can kick a ball and walk, you're on the kickball team. You can play competitive Skee-Ball in the arcade or compete in a macaroni and cheese cookoff. The possibilities are endless.

Now, you might say, "I don't have time to kick a ball or boogie; I'm busy." I feel you. We are all busy. But if you don't make room for joy in your life, then your life will be joyless, and it will end up sucking. You have to carve out the time for things that matter to you. Once you decide your joy is important, then prioritize it.

Your carefully crafted set of interests and activities reinforces your ability to validate yourself through the pursuit of your own goals. This makes you less likely to fall into the trap of seeking validation from someone else or looking to others to fill a sad, dark void. When you look to others to validate you or fill a void, you are more susceptible to getting manipulated. Instead, cultivate a fulfilling life of pursuits and joy that allows you to be happy on your own. This level of personal fulfillment creates the possibility of inviting another healthy, happy individual to join you and potentially merge your already satisfying lives.

Once you have your "thang," make it your routine. If you do Soul Cycle every Tuesday night, don't skip it to accept a first date. Establishing that you have a life and you prioritize self-care safeguards you from creating a void and giving up parts of yourself and sends valuable information about who you are right from the start. This information makes you more attractive and confident to others who perceive you as enjoying a fulfilling life. Yes, I am saying you should let that guy you just met understand that you'd rather ride a stationary bike in the dark with thirty strangers than go on a date with him next Tuesday. You'd love to go out with him, just not on Soul Cycle night. Or whatever your chosen thang is.

Avid dating on its own is not an acceptable "thang" because if all your time is spent trying to find someone else to complete your life, it means you are waiting for someone to come along and fill a void. It means your life is empty or lacks purpose, which is not inviting to other people. Some people go to work all day at their boring job and then come home to stare at their dating apps and set up dates all week long and have no other interests or hobbies whatsoever. I guarantee you, these people will never find a serious relationship. First of all, dating like it's your side hustle or like your life depends on it reeks of desperation. Second, if all you do is work, date, eat, and sleep on repeat (and that's it), you are boring as fuck. Bottom line, if all your free time is spent dating other people and not doing anything else, you will appear desperate and boring and nobody will want you. So, get a hobby already.

Compatibility

Whether you are seeking new friends or a person to date, the best place to meet people you are likely to be compatible with is where you are doing things that align with your interests. Do these things for yourself, to enhance your life, as mentioned earlier. But also do them for the added bonus that this is where you are likely to make good connections. If you're a vegan who loves to cook, sign up for plant-based cooking classes. If you're an art history major, hang out at museums, art galleries, and art walks. You get the point.

Compatibility is an important factor in relationship success. Consider some of the many ways people could be compatible:

Similar values about family, work, lifestyle, money, politics, religion, and world views. For example, we are both devout Christians who go to church every Sunday, or we are both atheists who don't believe in stories about a virgin who gave birth in a stable two thousand years ago.

Shared long-term goals, which might be a desire to make babies or maybe just rescue a bunch of street cats.

Physical attraction, which can be based on thousands of factors, conscious or unconscious, such as a subjective physical type, a fetish, chemistry, personality, personal history stored in the reptilian part of your brain, and even weird stuff like pheromones. (Here, I'm referring to the way a person's natural scent affects you on an unconscious level and how it influences how desirable you perceive the other person to be.)

Relational styles and personalities can be somewhat different, but they do need to fit together and be similar enough. For instance, introverts and extraverts can typically match well as long as they are not on the extreme ends of the scale. Sometimes someone appears to be one or the other but is actually what you call an "ambivert," which is in between extravert and introvert.

Interdependence

We often talk about independence and co-dependence as two extremes, but we rarely talk about the balanced middle ground of interdependence. Earlier chapters in this book have delved into co-dependence, which is a pattern of relying too heavily on others for feelings of self-worth and losing your core sense of self. By avoiding co-dependent patterns, we do want to become more independent but not *too* independent. The goal of a healthy relationship is interdependence.

Interdependence balances the self with others within a relationship. Both of you are working to meet each other's needs in ways that nourish the relationship while also allowing each other the space and freedom to be yourself and make decisions without guilt and fear. While shared activities keep people bonded, individuals in interdependent relationships also encourage each other to maintain separate hobbies or interests that exist outside the relationship.

My friend's husband told me that before he met her, he almost married the wrong girl. She used to text and call him multiple times throughout the day, track his location, and berate him for working late hours. His friends and his therapist helped him see that the relationship was toxic, and he eventually called off the engagement. When he met my awesome friend and they started talking about moving in together, he felt he should warn her that he often worked late during the week because he was starting his own business, which meant his hours could be unpredictable. He realized what a huge mistake he had almost made and how right this new relationship felt when her response was, *Yeah that's cool, I have plenty of things going on myself with yoga, my book club, and all the networking events that are part of my job.*

Interdependent couples understand that they will spend some time apart without making each other feel guilty for their separate pursuits while also enjoying quality time together. If you aren't already functioning well on your own or require someone else to make you feel complete, interdependence might feel like a new concept or a challenge. Likewise, if you're so independent to the point that you've convinced yourself you don't need anyone ever, then you're preventing a balanced interdependent relationship, too. The head bobbing, *I don't need no man* mentality is cool, as long as it's not rooted in fear of what happens when you become vulnerable to someone else.

You gotta love Cher, the iconic, sassy pop star who said it so well in an old interview from the '90s that has since gone viral on the internet. She said, "I love men. I think men are the coolest. But you don't really need them to live. My mom said to me, 'You know, sweetheart, one day you should settle down and marry a rich man.' And I said, 'Mom, I am a rich man.'" Boom! (Of course, we can't all be a "rich man" like Cher.) Then she adds this, which is a mentality worth considering: "My experience with men is great because I pick them because I like them. I don't need them."[3] This idea of wanting a person instead of needing a person shows how relationships work best as an addition to your already satisfying life.

Reciprocity

All relationships should be fairly reciprocal. Healthy relationships don't need to be perfectly reciprocal at all times, but they do need a sense of overall reciprocity. If you are friends with someone who never checks on you or reaches out ever, and you wonder what would happen if you stopped calling to keep it going, I recommend you stop calling. See what happens. If you never hear from this person again, that person

---

3   Cher, "Mom I Am a Rich Man," from Jane Pauley's 1996 interview with Cher, posted by the Cher Fan Club, https://www.youtube.com/watch?v=dZsL5R_CR-k.

wasn't your friend, or at least wasn't a very good one. If they do reach out to you eventually, then congratulations, you have just begun the process of recalibrating an imbalanced relationship. Now, chill the fuck out and let them come to you more often to create reciprocity. Trust me, the relationship will grow, and you will feel better when you are not the only one driving the friendship forward.

This notion of reciprocity applies to all relationships, including family and intimate partners, not just friends. Family relationships are sustained into adulthood when those relatives continue to earn your attention and affection, not just because you share the same bloodline. One of my clients was surprised and relieved to hear me validate her decision to stop calling her mother-in-law on her birthday after her divorce because this lady was always rude to her and sent her on a huge, annoying guilt trip after she filed for divorce from her cheating spouse. She said, "But isn't it rude of me to ignore an elderly relative on their birthday? I was raised to pay attention to elderly relatives." Paying attention to elderly relatives is a great value, but all adult relatives should be earning your attention; it does not need to be given automatically. If this lady makes you feel crummy every time you pick up the phone and listen to her snooty voice in your ear, then stop calling her.

As you create reciprocity in your personal life, think about who adds value and who seems to be sucking all the oxygen out of the room as soon as they enter. Who are the people supporting you, checking on you, listening to you, and showing they care about you? Those are the people you should continue to put energy toward. Put less energy toward the ones who talk and think only about themselves, who whine about everything that's wrong, who trash talk other people, who take and take but never give, who consistently flake or cancel, who frequently disappear, or who show little interest in you. Also limit your exposure to energy suckers, who are always there but somehow drain the life out of you. It is perfectly okay to stop meeting your sister for lunch if all she does is brag her brains out while gulping down caviar and then sits there as if she is suddenly paralyzed from the neck down when the bill comes. It is perfectly okay to distance yourself from odious relatives who don't add value or participate in healthy ways. If a relationship lacks reciprocity, it is not your job to hold it together at all costs.

Pick Your Battles

Some hills are not worth dying on. All relationships have problems. It doesn't even matter all that much what kinds of problems they are. What matters more is how well you can solve those problems together. Problem-solving starts with knowing which problems are worth trying to resolve, and which problems you're better off letting go of. Healthy, successful couples understand that there will always be some amount of conflict, and that's okay. He might never learn to chew his food with his mouth closed, and she might never stop talking on the phone at ear-splitting decibels. My guess is, at the end of the day, you'd still keep that person around, even if those things annoy the living shit out of you, right? So maybe quit bringing up the little stuff that definitely isn't going to make or break your rela-tionship. Sometimes, for the sake of your relationship, you have to let the little shit go.

Realistic Expectations

If you're hoping for a handsome young billionaire with a sparkling personality and no emotional baggage to sweep you off your feet, you will probably hope forever. If you only swipe on men who are over six feet tall or have beards or whatever your physical criteria may be, you might be missing out on a real connection with a great guy who's five feet, eleven inches tall or shaves his face once in a while.

And also, if you are hoping that the person you are with will suddenly change and start meeting your needs after you've told him what they are repeatedly and nothing ever changes, you will also hope forever. The information in this book so far should be giving you a good amount of clarity to see the person without rose-colored goggles or trauma brain—see them for who they are, so you can determine what is realistic. Since nobody is perfect, only you know what you are willing to tolerate in another human being. You must be honest with yourself about how you really feel and what it is doing to you. Let's say your fiancé is a die-hard mama's boy, and it's not getting any better. Reflect on what your future life with your man and his mama is going to look like, and decide whether it's something you can put up with forever or not. Be honest. You are the only one who knows the answer to that.

Avoid Becoming a Target While Dating

Dating is tough, especially in today's digital age. Both men and women can be manipulators, and you will find them in both heterosexual and LGBTQ relationships. Relationships with narcissists, manipulators, and emotional predators usually start off exciting and then quickly become tumultuous.

DATING APP AWARENESS

Dating apps can be a great tool when used the right way. They show you who's out there right away, allowing you to instantaneously connect with other singles in your area, which can be a lot of fun. Here's where expectations can impact your enjoyment factor. Are you using this tool to find your future spouse as soon as possible? Are you hoping you will swipe right on the future love of your life before you grow one more gray hair on your head?

Yikes, the pressure. The dating app device was not built for that.

It's a numbers game; look at a few hundred people, swipe on fifty to one hundred, and who knows, maybe you will find your lucky winner. It's a needle in a fuckin' haystack, but it's dark out and you forgot your glasses. It's a bargain-basement dig-through-the-messy-hodgepodge clearance rack and just maybe, if you're lucky, you will find that gem of a sweater you've always been looking for. If you're extra lucky, it will be your size, without a cigarette hole in the sleeve. That's what looking for a serious relationship on a dating app is like, so if you understand and accept that concept, then jump in and play.

Let's look at the expectations factor. Maybe you would love to find a serious, long-term relationship. Fair enough, but what you have in front of you is a device with stats. While sifting through a variety of profiles, evaluate not only how cute they look in their photo, but also what they are choosing (or not choosing) to share about themselves. Immediately swipe left on anyone presenting a bathroom mirror selfie without any other information than their height and age. Read what they've written about themselves and select people with whom you think you'd enjoy talking, regardless of how attractive they look in their photo because two-dimensional imaging can only tell you so much. I'm not saying you should strike up a conversation with the Hunchback of Notre Dame so you can talk about your mutual interest in poetry. I'm saying don't limit your swipes to your standard type or hottest-looking person, and instead investigate the ones who appear interesting to meet and talk to.

If it turns out, through texting and talking, that you do enjoy chatting with this person, great, keep that going as long as you can. Don't just meet up with some cute stranger who asks you out for a drink right away. It's a total waste of your time, energy, makeup, gas, calories, money, and effort if they turn out to be a drone, a dickhead, or an egomaniac. I can't stress enough how important it is to be picky about who you decide to meet in person.

Also, once you have built up some level of rapport through your chats, meeting each other will feel that much more familiar, fun, and exciting. It eliminates some of the jitters and awkwardness of meeting a new person. Conversing ahead of time sets you up to have a great outing because you are meeting someone you already know you enjoy interacting with, regardless of whether you'll be attracted to one another. And if the attraction is not there, that's okay, you had a nice time with a cool person. Connecting with other cool, positive people is never a waste of time, whether it turns into romance or not. Your social time should be about surrounding yourself with positive energy.

A word of warning. Dating apps are ripe playing fields for people who want to hide who they really are and entice unwitting subjects into relationships. Some people are seeking someone who is vulnerable and naïve, who is more likely to fall for their bullshit and give them what they want. How do you make sure that's not you? Now that we've talked about how they present themselves, let's talk about how you are presenting yourself.

Make sure nothing in your profile reeks of a wounded bird. You might be sick of some fuckboy's shit, but do not mention that you are sick of any bad boy behavior. That indicates you've been fooled before, so chances are pretty high you can be fooled again. This includes sounding resentful, bitter, cynical, and "over it" because those attitudes imply that you've been a sucker before and now you're broken inside, which suggests you might be easy to take advantage of.

You do, however, want to sound positive, upbeat, independent, and like you're living your best life. That said, don't announce stuff like, "I tend to see the best in everyone!" because again, you're basically telling narcissists, manipulators, and con artists that you are trusting and that your antennae for bullshit is defective. You are convincing them that you are the kind of person who will ignore their unsavory or suspicious behavior and make excuses for them. The perfect girl! Here are a few other things you might not want to include in your profile or share immediately because they might make you a potential target:

- You want kids ASAP (so they can pretend they want them too and reel you in hook, line, and sinker).

- You have been single for a long time (a sign you might be desperate).

- You have been married multiple times (a sign you trust all the wrong people).

- You have wealth (something to potentially steal).

- You talk too soon about a toxic ex-partner (you are emotionally raw and easy to manipulate or take advantage of).

- You overshare anything extremely personal. (For example, maybe don't tell them things like you are saving up for a boob job or your little brother spent time in jail.)

- You allude to having been mistreated or abused. (This makes it too easy for them to imagine having their turn with you.)

- You mention how hard finding the right person has been for you or that you have met nothing but jerks. (This reads as vulnerable, desperate, and ready to get mistreated again.)

- You reveal wild, impulsive, or risk-taking behavior. (These behaviors suggest you are interested in or open to things that friends and family might caution you against.)

FIRST DATE RED FLAGS

Now that you've landed a first date, how do you make sure he's not a narcissist, manipulator, or some kind of emotional predator? Here are a few dead giveaways.

Watch out for immediate love bombing. The first date is way too soon for a reasonable person to divulge that you are the most beautiful and incredible person they've ever met. It is way too soon for them to know, or at least tell you that they know, that you are the one and they want a commitment with you. This tends to be the strategy of a manipulator who wants to get you hooked on them. They want you to become addicted to those delicious feelings they invoke. That way, when they begin to mistreat you, you're in such a state of disbelief that you literally don't believe this could be the same person.

Notice whether they ask you any questions about you or talk exclusively and incessantly about themselves. Narcissists are always on stage. Everything is a performance. You will see the signs of a narcissist if your first meeting is their way of proving to you right out of the gate how amazing they are, and they leave knowing very little about you. My friend, hoping to meet someone intelligent, went on a first date with a rocket scientist who spent the entire afternoon talking about every single person he had ever dated and why they weren't good enough for him. Yawn. Watch out for guys like Billy the Grandstander, if you remember this character from chapter 3 on Egomaniacs. He is the one who rattles off his long, impressive resume the moment you meet him to prove how extraordinary he is, but once he has you on the hook, he's sliding into your wallet like a slippery snake, sucking you dry.

On the flip side, other manipulators might strategically remain vague and question you to learn how to better manipulate you as they share very little about themselves. They will tell you snippets of what you need to know. If they refuse to talk about their family at all or remain vague about their personal history, be suspicious of that, too. If they are vague about what they do for a living, or if their "work" sounds extremely confusing, that should raise an eyebrow. Pay attention to inconsistent stories in which they contradict themselves and when things don't add up.

Anyone who invites you to dinner, promising to take you out, and then oopsies, forgets their wallet at home and asks you to pay this time, should raise a huge red flag. Some people do this for sport, basking in all the free meals they can get. What are the odds that a person would plan a date with someone they are excited to see and then forget to bring their wallet? Come on. Also, that behavior is so Anna Delvey, our favorite fake "German heiress" criminal, whose credit cards frequently malfunctioned when she invited people to lavish dinners and luxurious vacations.

Manipulators and toxic people, on the first date or quickly there-after, might rant excessively about past relationships, labeling their ex-partners as crazy. This indicates many things about this person: they like to play the victim, they are attracted to drama, they blame and gaslight everyone else without taking responsibility for their own behavior, or all of the above. It is, of course, possible that this person has actually been the victim of emotional abuse, but if that's true, they are unlikely to feel comfortable sharing those details with someone they just met. It is also possible that they are some sort of victim of abuse but also emotionally unstable and perpetually attracted to drama and chaos, which is still a red flag because that dynamic is not healthy to be around.

When making new connections, be mindful of the kind of energy you want to create and surround yourself with. Anyone who doesn't match that energy is not worthy of your time and effort.

Remember this:

You are who you surround yourself with: So stay away from the negative, whiney, sad sacks who suck the energy out of you.

Chapter 14

YOUR FORTRESS: AN ASSHOLE-FREE ZONE

ASSHOLES ARE EVERYWHERE! But that doesn't mean you have to put up with them. The best way to ensure an environment free of assholes, toxic people, narcissists, and manipulators is to be the kind of person they don't want to be around. When you know what you want and when you are comfortable in your skin, you become a person that is hard to manipulate. The person who doesn't get rattled by the asshole's demands and doesn't buy their bullshit is probably not on their favorites list.

The new and improved version of you is more self-aware and grows more self-aware every day. You are never finished learning about yourself. Along the way, you will likely experience life lessons that test you and push you harder. Some experiences might feel like setbacks or relapses, but remember, it is not a straight line to the top. Everyone's journey gets a little messy.

Recovery Can Be Messy in the Middle

Somewhere, a therapist is battling her own issues. Therapists often become therapists to understand and work out their own family dysfunction or psychological issues. Not surprisingly, they end up specializing in disorders that run in their families.

My friend Jan is one of them. Her single, alcoholic mother was emotionally abusive to her and her sister, Nikki, who was eventually diagnosed with borderline personality disorder. Surprisingly, as the girls grew into adulthood, Jan's mother was not her worst abuser; it was her sister, whose attention-seeking behavior spiraled out of control. Nikki manipulated Jan and everyone around them, constantly posing as the victim and the martyr. Jan remembers feeling terrorized and trapped by the harrowing threat of what Nikki might do if she didn't get her way. She often gave in to Nikki's outrageous demands to avoid conflict, keep the peace, and stay safe. That still didn't stop the sisters from fighting often and hard as Jan would try to explain her side. But her words would go through one ear and out the other. Her side never mattered. Jan didn't realize that they could never have a normal sibling relationship until the day she learned about her sister's disorder in a classroom in graduate school. That is when she realized she couldn't fix her, help her, change her, or have any normal relationship with her.

Jan did a lot of work in her own therapy to overcome the trauma of her family dysfunction. She regularly attended Al-Anon meetings. Al-Anon is a twelve-step program for people who are affected by someone else's drinking. It is also helpful for people who are affected by someone else's disorder or unhealthy behavior. Jan began to understand that she succumbed to co-dependency patterns with other people too, as she was so used to circumventing and people-pleasing the difficult, toxic people in her life in order to stay safe.

Once she became a therapist, Jan felt she understood her clients who struggled with her sister's disorder. She wanted to help them with compassion and empathy in a therapeutic setting. This may have been her way of also helping her clients' loved ones, people she never met but felt she deeply understood.

When Tina showed up in her office, she quickly formed a connection with Jan. She would tell Jan that she wished she could find a friend like her. She would schedule the latest appointment Jan had and invite her for dinner or drinks with her after their session. Jan, who had come a long way in setting boundaries, upheld her therapeutic boundary. She explained with compassion that the nature of their therapeutic relationship restricted outside personal time together. Tina persisted. Sometimes she became emotional and would argue, "That rule is bullshit!" She would schedule more than one session a week and ask for late-night phone sessions, and then break down in tears saying she couldn't afford this much therapy. She talked about wanting to kill herself and that she needed to know Jan truly cared about her, accusing her of just wanting to make money off her. Jan finally offered to find her resources for a higher level of care, which incited an emotional outburst and feelings of abandonment.

It was only a matter of time before Jan began to slowly violate her own boundaries by accepting Tina's phone calls after she had terminated treatment. Jan spent hours on the phone with Tina while she was in crisis, without charging her, desperately trying to reassure her. She found herself promising that she would not abandon her. Jan's boundaries melted away, and she invited Tina to stay connected and update her while seeking alternate treatment. This resulted in Tina calling, texting, and asking to swing by her office regularly. Jan finally stopped fighting the friendship Tina wanted so badly. Almost every day, Jan received texts from Tina asking to "chat," which essentially resulted in free therapy for Tina. She called Jan her best friend. At the end of a long, draining workday with clients, she took Tina's phone calls about her problem of the day, and sometimes about wanting to end her life.

Jan naturally became overwhelmed, and finally realized what she had gotten herself into by extending herself outside the bounds of therapy. She didn't understand how she could have tossed her boundaries aside and gotten pulled into something she knew was wrong but also felt so . . . familiar. Once again, feeling bombarded with threats, drama, and volatility, Jan had been triggered, reverted back to her baseline, and done what felt familiar to her, which was to take care of the sick person's feelings to the point of self-neglect. She lost herself by caring too much. She ignored her own boundaries to spare the feelings of someone emotionally unstable. She gave in, acquiesced, rescued, and avoided disappointing the other person at all costs.

"I guess I just thought maybe I could help her better as a 'friend' than as her therapist," she told me.

"Why would that be? You're a good therapist, Jan."

"I don't know. Maybe because that's what *she* wanted. I thought maybe my friendship was what she needed."

"Is that what *you* needed?" I pushed back. "Did you really need a friend to help and fix?"

"No," she admitted. "I got pulled into giving her what she convinced me she needed, whether it was actually healthy or not." As Jan said this and reflected on what happened, she realized that her co-dependent tendencies were reawakened with this client.

Self-awareness is only the first step. The next step is to constantly practice attunement to what is happening around you and inside you. Practice noticing what happens in your body when you are around a particular person. For example, Jan's stomach would tighten into knots when Tina's name popped up on her phone. When people make you feel tense, pay attention to that sensation and reflect on what they are bringing up inside you.

Jan realized that she needed to confront Tina and set her boundaries more firmly. Jan carefully explained to Tina that from the start she had not been comfortable having a friendship together and that she had made a mistake allowing it. Tina had a hard time understanding Jan's boundary and pushed back intensely, spiraling in a variety of directions. She threatened suicide once again, insisting that Jan was the reason she was alive and that she couldn't go on without her in her life. Tina became angry and screamed at Jan. She cried, she accepted it for a moment, and then she circled back to needing to talk more and more, over and over again. She repeatedly demanded a last "closure" conversation. Jan, exhausted and rattled to the core, finally decided to stop all contact. Tina continued to call, send gifts, and leave messages begging to talk. Tina accused Jan of lacking empathy and made vague threats about her professional license. Jan practiced detachment by not responding, which wasn't easy and required many deep breaths.

When you experience setbacks, don't beat yourself up. It is simply the universe sending you a pop quiz to make sure you're on top of your game and not slipping up. If you do slip up, it's a life lesson to keep you on your toes so you'll do better next time. If you learn from that lesson, you will do better next time. Life is just a series of journeys teaching us to be the best versions of ourselves. Let those lessons shape you into someone stronger moving forward.

Not Everyone Is an Asshole

There will be times when the person is not an asshole or a narcissist or a terrible person or anything other than another human being with their own issues and baggage that somehow clashes with yours. Your own self-awareness will help you navigate this.

When someone is hurting you, draining you, upsetting you, or making you uncomfortable in any way, it is up to you to identify what you're feeling and express that to the other person without assigning blame. Ask for what you need. Set the boundaries. Then see what happens. If the person doesn't listen to you, or if they can't or won't give you what you need, then step back and evaluate how important it is to keep this person in your life. Sometimes nobody is the asshole in a relationship but the two people are not compatible or healthy together. Or maybe you've changed your mind about maintaining a friendship or you've outgrown a long-term relationship. This can make you feel sad and provoke feelings of guilt, but you are allowed to evolve and decide that some people don't match the kind of energy you are trying to create in your life.

This idea was especially hard for Lexi, who got married to Sean when she was twenty-seven years old, fully understanding that she had made a vow to be together forever. Sean was a really nice guy, too. By the time Lexi turned thirty, they had brought their little nugget, Luke, into the world. Everything seemed great. Sean worked hard and devoted time and energy to Luke, teaching him sports as soon as he could walk, signing him up for Little League, and showing up at every game. His devotion and stability were the things that had attracted Lexi to Sean in the first place, as she had come from a dysfunctional family with an alcoholic father who was often absent or volatile.

Lexi did a lot of growing during their marriage; she went to therapy to heal from her turbulent family history, attended Al-Anon, and blossomed professionally after returning to work following maternity leave. Over time, her dynamic with Sean grew into something that felt to her like two roommates raising a child. Sean was never a big talker and didn't like to chat, go out, or socialize much. This left Lexi, an extreme extravert, feeling lonely in their relationship together. Many things stopped aligning for them. The couple grew increasingly distant, even to the point of sleeping in separate rooms. Lexi tried to rev things up with date nights and everything else recommended by therapists, but their relationship remained emotionally distant. As a result of her own increased self-awareness and personal growth, Lexi came to realize that she had married a really good person who didn't feel like the right match for her as a partner. This realization tore her up with guilt and kept her paralyzed in a marriage that lacked compatibility for several years. "How do you leave a nice guy like Sean?" she would repeat to her friends who questioned her happiness.

Giving herself permission to be honest with herself and honor her true feelings is what finally gave Lexi the courage to talk to Sean about an amicable divorce. She realized that not only was it important for her to manifest the life she craved, but also that Sean deserved to find someone more compatible with him. She was doing him no favors by going through the motions together. It was a bumpy road at first, but today, years later, they are both happily remarried, and Luke is a happy tween with two great homes, four awesome parents, and not much to complain about.

Always remember that when the twin demons of guilt and shame are holding you back, you can deconstruct them by questioning your expectations and asking yourself how realistic or sustainable your expectations are. Our unnecessary expectations are often the cause of our own misery. In this case, Lexi set herself free from the expectation of staying with the same person forever when feelings change. Instead, she honored her true feelings, and it worked out fantastically.

This example illustrates how hard it can be to give value to our own thoughts and feelings. Some people struggle with leaving a real, certified, world-class asshole because they feel guilty denying their vow or even hurting that toxic person's feelings. Imagine that—feeling guilty for leaving someone who is harming you. And yet I'm sure many people reading this book either have or are currently struggling with that exact problem. I wrote this book mostly for them. In those cases, I try to help them see that they are not a bad person for leaving someone abominable, and when they still don't buy it, I tell them about Lexi. I tell them that even leaving a good, kind person who doesn't make you happy does not make you a bad person; it makes you an honest, genuine person who knows how to take care of yourself.

There is Always Going to Be a New Asshole.

Brazilian jiu-jitsu philosophy is also about infinite learning. Nobody ever gets to a point at which they have mastered everything there is to know. You will often see the highest-ranked black belts not only teaching but also still learning, still devouring new techniques. There will always be a new tactic, some crazy shit you've never seen before. If someone beats you, you did not lose; you learned what you need to work on. As Grand Master Carlos Gracie puts it, "There is no losing in jiu jitsu. You either win or you learn." This philosophy applies to life. Take every disappointment as an opportunity to learn without shame in failure.

Recovery is always full of challenges. Each person's path is rarely a straight line to the top, and your path will most likely include a series of obstacles and setbacks that move you in different directions, sometimes forward, backward, or in circles. We don't build strength without struggle, fight, and perseverance. Nobody gets the world champion title without getting punched in the face a few times first. This struggle, this path, this life—all of it—is uniquely yours. Don't let it defeat you or wear you down. Let it instead reveal what you're capable of as you heal and grow and become the person you are truly meant to be.

At all times, remember who you are, who you want to be, and who you are becoming. I hope you are now very much aware of your needs and desires, as well as what your trigger buttons are, and that you know when they are getting pushed. You do not sacrifice yourself to protect fragile egos. You don't believe everything the egomaniac says, because it's usually nonsense. You remain careful about who you confide in or where you share your secrets, knowing that potential predators are salivating at the thought of your weaknesses revealed. You put energy into reciprocal relationships based on mutual trust, respect, and support, instead of squandering it on emotional vampires who leave you empty. You trust your intuition and *your own* version of reality. You set boundaries and consistently maintain them. You project confidence. You are resilient. You stay out of other people's heads. You don't take things so personally. You successfully blend compassion with firmness. You remain connected to who you are and what you value. You demonstrate bland indifference when egomaniacs, narcissists, master manipulators, and all different kinds of assholes try to push your buttons.

All of this does not make you cold, uncaring, or selfish; you are now just harder to manipulate.

ACKNOWLEDGMENTS

THANK YOU TO MY CLIENTS for trusting me with the most intimate details of their lives, which have helped shape the stories in this book.

Thank you to Maggie Langrick, Eva Avery, and Jen Jensen at Wonderwell, who helped me envision the book I wanted to write. They encouraged me to bring my voice to life on the page while convincing me that my voice was unique and interesting enough to attract readers. Thank you to the entire team at Greenleaf for your guidance and professional polish, especially my editor Sally Garland.

Thank you to my husband, Tony, who supported my vision from the start and believed, without hesitation, that I could pull this off. Thank you to my daughter, Chloe, the sweetest cheerleader.

Thank you to my mom, who remains unconditionally and unwaveringly proud of me, no matter what, even throughout my more questionable moments. Thank you to my late father for the wisdom he gave me, which is infused throughout my work.

Thank you to my friends and colleagues, who believe in me and seem to actually enjoy reading and listening to my every word on this topic and more.

Thank you to my readers for choosing to read what a potty-mouthed, straight-shooter therapist has to say about the unfortunate assholes out there.

ABOUT THE AUTHOR

CARLA LITTO, MA, LMFT, is a licensed marriage and family therapist with two master degrees in psychology and a successful private practice in Los Angeles, California, who helps many people improve their personal relationships and transform their lives. Using her detective skills and keen manipulation radar, she is known as the "tell-it-like-it-is" therapist who cuts right through the bullshit to help her "stuck" clients get unstuck. Carla is happily married with more cats than kids. In her down time, she enjoys practicing Brazilian jiu-jitsu, watching stand-up comedy, and eating pizza.